Cornish Legends

20p

For further information of all the titles in this series please visit:-
www.tormark.co.uk

The stories collected here were first published in *Cornish Legends*
and *Demons, Ghosts and Spectres*

Published by Tor Mark, United Downs Ind Est, Redruth, Cornwall TR16 5HY

First published 2008
This reprint 2010

Cover illustration by Linda Garland
Designed by Alix Wood – www.alixwood.co.uk

ISBN 978 085025 409 9

Printed by R Booth Ltd, The Praze, Penryn, Cornwall TR10 8AA

Introduction

The stories collected here are taken from Robert Hunt's *Popular Romances of the West of England*, published in 1865.

Hunt was the posthumous son of a naval captain and was born in 1807 at Devonport, then called Plymouth Dock. He went to school in Plymouth and Penzance, then was apprenticed to a surgeon in London. He practised as a physician for five years; while in his early twenties suffered a serious breakdown and resolved to convalesce in the West Country and 'to visit each relic of Old Cornwall and to gather up every existing tale of its ancient people'.

As a child he had visited Bodmin with his mother and heard tales of Hender the huntsman of Lanhydrock and legends of a devil who had played strange pranks with a tower that stands on a neighbouring hill. The notebook in which he had recorded these tales had been lost, and when he returned to recover the tales, the memory had gone from the people and these tales were lost for ever.

Determined that no further 'drolls and romances' should be lost, for ten months he roamed Cornwall and the borders of Dartmoor sitting at the hearths of the country people or in close companionship with the miners, 'drinking deeply from the stream of legendary lore which was at that time flowing as from a well of living water.' He also met possibly the last two wandering story tellers then in Cornwall. Uncle Anthony James was a blind man from Cury who spent his whole year on the road, calling regularly at the same time of year. For a night's lodging and food he would entertain the company with ballads and stories, accompanying himself on the fiddle. The other was Billy Frost of St Just, who used to go the rounds of the feasts in the neighbourhood and be 'well entertained at the public houses for the sake of his drolls'.

Thirty years were to pass between this first collection and the publication of Hunt's work. In that time Hunt established himself as an important scientific writer and a Fellow of the Royal Society, founded a Mechanics' Institute in Plymouth, became a lecturer and later professor at the Royal School of Mines as well as President of the Cornwall Polytechnic Society, and was for 37 years keeper of mining records for the county. In the latter capacity he was able to tour the county, adding to his stock of tales and folk-lore. His most important technical work was British Mining, a monumental survey of the industry published in 1884, three years before his death.

Hunt acknowledged the help he received from many people in his compilation of Cornish legends, including William Bottrell who was to publish his own collection in three volumes as *Traditions and Hearthside Stories of West Cornwall*, between 1870 and 1880.

The Demon Tregeagle

Who has not heard of the wild spirit Tregeagle? He haunts equally the moor, the rocky coasts, and the blown sandhills of Cornwall. From north to south, from east to west, this doomed spirit is heard of, and to the day of judgement he is doomed to wander, pursued by avenging fiends – for ever endeavouring to perform some task by which he hopes to secure repose, and being for ever defeated.

Who has not heard the howling of Tregeagle? When the storms come with all their strength from the Atlantic, and urge themselves upon the rocks around the Land's End, the howls of the spirit are louder than the roaring of the winds. When calms rest upon the ocean, and the waves can scarcely form upon the resting waters, low wailings creep along the coast. These are the wailings of this wandering soul. When midnight is on the moor or on the mountains, and the night winds whistle amidst the rugged cairns, the shrieks of Tregeagle are distinctly heard. We know then that he is being pursued by the demon dogs, and that till daybreak he must fly with all speed before them. The voice of Tregeagle is everywhere, and yet he is unseen by human eye.

There are some men who appear to be from their births given over to the will of tormenting demons. Such a man was Tregeagle, a man diabolically wicked. He seems to have been urged on from one crime to another until the cup of sin was overflowing.

Tregeagle was wealthy beyond most men of his time, and his wealth purchased for him that immunity which the Church, in her degenerate days, too often accorded to those who could aid, with their gold or power, the sensual priesthood. As a magistrate, he was tyrannical and unjust, and many an innocent man was wantonly sacrificed by him for the purpose of hiding his own dark deeds. As a landlord, he was rapacious and unscrupulous, and frequently so involved his tenants in his toils that they could not escape his grasp. The stain of secret murder clings to his memory, and he is said to have sacrificed his sister whose goodness stood between him and his demon passions; his wife and children perished victims to his cruelties. At length death drew near to relieve the land of a monster whose name was a terror to all who heard it. Devils waited to secure the soul they had won, and Tregeagle in

5

terror gave to the priesthood wealth, that they might fight with them and save his soul from eternal fire. Desperate was the struggle, but the powerful exorcisms of the banded brotherhood of a neighbouring monastery drove back the evil ones, and Tregeagle slept with his fathers, safe in the custody of the churchmen, who buried him with high honours in St Breock church. They sang chants and read prayers above his grave, to secure the soul which they thought they had saved. But Tregeagle was not fated to rest. Satan desired still to gain possession of such a gigantic sinner, and we can only refer what ensued to the influence of the wicked spiritings of his ministers.

A dispute arose between two wealthy families respecting the ownership of extensive lands around Bodmin. The question had been rendered more difficult by the nefarious conduct of Tregeagle, who had acted as steward to one of the claimants, and who had destroyed ancient deeds, forged others, and indeed made it appear that he was the real proprietor of the domain. Large portions of the land Tregeagle had sold, and other parts were leased upon long terms, he having received all the money and appropriated it. His death led to inquiries, and then the transactions were gradually brought to light. Involving, as this did, large sums of money – and indeed it was a question upon which turned the future well-being or ruin of a family – it was fought by the lawyers with great pertinacity. The legal questions had been argued several times before the judges at the assizes. The trials had been deferred, new trials had been sought for and granted, and every possible plan known to the lawyers for postponing the settlement of a suit had been tried. A day was at length fixed upon which a final decision must be come to, and a special jury was sworn to administer justice between the contending parties. Witnesses innumerable were examined as to the validity of a certain deed, and the balance of evidence was equally suspended. The judge was about to sum up the case and refer the question to the jury, when the defendant in the case, coming to court, proclaimed aloud that he had yet another witness to produce. There was a strange silence in the judgement-hall. It was felt that something chilling to the soul was amongst them, and there was a simultaneous throb of terror as Tregeagle was led into the witness-box.

When the awe-struck assembly had recovered, the lawyers for the defendant commenced their examination, which was long and terrible. The result, however, was the disclosure of an involved system of fraud, of which the honest defendant had been the victim, and the jury unhesitatingly gave a verdict in his favour.

The trial over, everyone expected to see the spectre-witness removed. There, however, he stood, powerless to fly, although he evidently desired to do so. Spirits of darkness were waiting to bear him away, but some spell of holiness prevented them from touching him. There was a struggle with the good and the evil angels for the sinner's soul, and the assembled court appeared frozen with horror. At length the judge with dignity commanded the defendant to remove his witness.

'To bring him from the grave has been to me so dreadful a task, that I leave him to your care, and that of the Prior, by whom he was so beloved.' Having said this, the defendant left the court.

The churchmen were called in, and long were the deliberations between them and the lawyers, as to the best mode of disposing with Tregeagle.

They could resign him to the devil at once, but by long trial the worst of crimes might be absolved, and as good churchmen they could not sacrifice a human soul. The only thing was to give the spirit some task, difficult beyond the power of human nature, which might be extended far into eternity.

Time might thus gradually soften the obdurate soul, which still retained all the black dyes of the sins done in the flesh, that by infinitely slow degrees repentance might exert its softening power. The spell therefore put upon Tregeagle was, that as long as he was employed on some endless assigned task, there should be some hope of salvation, and that he should be secured from the assaults of the devil as long as he laboured steadily. A moment's rest was fatal – labour unresting, and for ever, was his doom.

One of the lawyers, remembering that Dozmary Pool was bottomless, and that a thorn bush, which had been flung into it but a few weeks before, had made its appearance in Falmouth Harbour, proposed that Tregeagle might be employed to empty this profound lake.

Then one of the churchmen, to make the task yet more enduring, proposed that it should be performed by the aid of a limpet-shell having a hole in it. This was agreed to and the required incantations were duly made. Bound by mystical spells, Tregeagle was removed to the dark moors and duly set to work. Year after year passed by, and there, day and night, summer and winter, storm and shine, Tregeagle was bending over the dark water working hard with his perforated shell; yet the pool remained at the same level.

His old enemy the devil kept a careful eye on the doomed one, resolving, if possible, to secure so choice an example of evil. Often did he raise tempests sufficiently wild, as he supposed, to drive Tregeagle from his work, knowing that if he failed for a season to labour he could seize and secure him. These were long tried in vain, but at length an auspicious hour presented itself.

Nature was at war with herself, the elements had lost their balance, and there was a terrific struggle to recover it. Lightnings flashed and coiled like fiery snakes around the rocks of Roughtor. Fire-balls fell on the desert moors and hissed in the accursed lake. Thunders pealed through the heavens, and echoed from hill to hill; an earthquake shook the solid earth, and terror was on all living. The winds arose and raged with a fury which was irresistible, and hail beat so mercilessly on all things that it spread death around. Long did Tregeagle stand the 'pelting of the pitiless storm', but at length he yielded to its force and fled. The demons in crowds were at his heels. He doubled, however, on his pursuers and returned to the lake; but so rapid were they that he could not rest the required moment to dip his shell in the now seething waters.

Three times he fled round the lake, and the evil ones pursued him. Then, feeling that there was no safety for him near Dozmary Pool, he sprang swifter than the wind across it, shrieking with agony, and thus – since the devils cannot cross water, and were obliged to go round the lake – he gained on them and fled over the moor.

Away, away went Tregeagle, faster and faster the dark spirits pursuing, and they had nearly overtaken him when he saw Roche Rock and its chapel before him. He rushed up the rocks, with giant power clambered to the eastern window, and dashed his head through it, thus securing the shelter of its sanctity. The defeated demons retired, and long and loud were their wild wailings in the air. The inhabitants of the moors and of the neighbouring towns slept not a wink that night.

Tregeagle was safe, his head was within the holy church, though his body was exposed on a bare rock to the storm. Earnest were the prayers of the blessed hermit in his cell on the rock to be relieved from his nocturnal and sinful visitor.

In vain were the recluse's prayers. Day after day as he knelt at the altar, the ghastly head of the doomed sinner grinned horridly down upon him. Every holy ejaculation fell upon Tregeagle's ear like molten iron. He writhed and shrieked under the torture; but legions of devils filled the air, ready to seize him, if for a moment he withdrew his head from the sanctuary. Sabbath after sabbath the little chapel on the rock was rendered a scene of sad confusion by the interruptions which Tregeagle caused. Men trembled with fear at his agonising cries, and women swooned. At length the place was deserted, and even the saint of the rock was wasting to death by the constant perturbation in which he was kept by the unholy spirit, and the demons who, like carrion birds, swarmed around the holy cairn. Things could not go on thus. The monks of Bodmin and the priests from the neighbouring churches gathered together, and the result of their long and anxious deliberations was that Tregeagle, guarded by two saints, should be taken to the north coast near Padstow and employed in making trusses of sand, and ropes of sand with which to bind them. By powerful spell Tregeagle was removed from Roche, and fixed upon the sandy shores of the Padstow district. Sinners are seldom permitted to enjoy any peace of soul. As the ball of sand grew in form, the tides rose and the breakers spread out the sands again a level sheet; again it was packed together and again washed away. Toil! toil! toil! day and night unrestingly, sand on sand grew with each hour, and ruthlessly the ball was swept, by one blow of the sea wave, along the shore.

The cries of Tregeagle were dreadful; and as the destruction of the sand heap was constantly recurring, a constantly increasing despair gained the mastery over hope, and the ravings of the baffled soul were louder than the roarings of the winter tempest.

Baffled in making trusses of sand, Tregeagle seized upon the loose particles and began to spin them into a rope. Long and patiently did he pursue his task, and hope once more rose like a star out of the midnight darkness of despair. A rope was forming, when a storm came up with all its fury from the Atlantic and swept the particles of sand away over the hills.

The inhabitants of Padstow had seldom any rest. At every tide the howlings of Tregeagle banished sleep from each eye. But now so fearful were the sounds of the doomed soul, in the madness of the struggle between hope and despair, that the people fled the town, and clustered upon the neighbouring plains, praying, as with one voice, to be relieved from the sad presence of this monster.

St Petrock, moved by the tears and petitions of the people, resolved to remove the spirit; and by the intense earnestness of his prayers, after long wrestling, he subdued Tregeagle to his will. Having chained him with the bonds which the saint had formed with his own hands, every link of which had been welded with a prayer, St Petrock led the spirit away from the north coast and stealthily placed him on the southern shores.

In those days Ella's Town, now Helston, was a flourishing port. Ships sailed into the estuary, up to the town, and they brought all sorts of merchandise, and returned with cargoes of tin from the mines of Breage and Wendron.

The wily monk placed his charge at Bareppa and there condemned him to carry sacks of sand across the estuary of the Loe, and to empty them at Porthleven until the beach was clean down to the rocks. The priest was a good observer. He knew that the sweep of the tide was from Trewavas Head round the coast towards the Lizard, and that the sand would be carried back steadily and speedily as fast as the spirit could remove it.

Long did Tregeagle labour; and, of course, in vain. His struggles were giant-like to perform his task, but he saw the sands return as regularly as he removed them. The sufferings of the poor fishermen who inhabited the coast around Porthleven were great. As the howlings of Tregeagle disturbed the dwellers in Padstow, so did they now distress those toil-worn men.

A mischievous demon watcher, in pure wantonness, brought relief to those fishers of the sea.

Tregeagle was laden with a sack of sand of enormous size, and was wading across the mouth of the estuary, when one of those wicked devils, who were kept ever near Tregeagle, in very idleness tripped up the heavily laden spirit. The sea was raging with the irritation of a passing storm; and as Tregeagle fell the sack was seized by the waves and its contents poured out across this arm of the sea.

There, to this day it rests, a bar of sand, fatally destroying the harbour of Ella's Town. The rage of the inhabitants of this sea-port – now destroyed – was great; and with all their priests, away they went to the Loe Bar, and assailed their destroyer. Against human anger Tregeagle was proof. The shock of tongues fell harmlessly on his ear, and the assault of human weapons was unavailing.

By the aid of the priests, and faith-inspired prayers, the bonds were once more placed upon Tregeagle; and he was, by the force of bell, book and candle, sent to the Land's End. There he would find no harbour to destroy and but few people to terrify. His task was to sweep the sand from Porthcurnow Cove round the headland called Tol-Pedn-Penwith into Nanjizal Cove. Those who know that rugged headland, with its cubical masses of granite piled in Titanic grandeur one upon another, will appreciate the task; and when to all the difficulties are added the strong sweep of the Atlantic current – that portion of the Gulf Stream which washes our southern shores – it will be evident that the melancholy spirit has, indeed, a task which must endure until the world shall end.

Even until today is Tregeagle labouring at his task. In calms his wailing is heard; and those sounds which some call the 'soughing of the wind' are known to be the moanings of Tregeagle; while the coming storms are predicted by the fearful moanings of this condemned mortal.

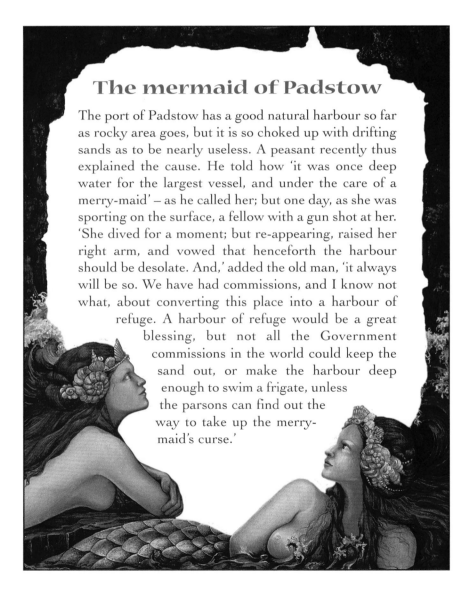

The mermaid of Padstow

The port of Padstow has a good natural harbour so far as rocky area goes, but it is so choked up with drifting sands as to be nearly useless. A peasant recently thus explained the cause. He told how 'it was once deep water for the largest vessel, and under the care of a merry-maid' – as he called her; but one day, as she was sporting on the surface, a fellow with a gun shot at her. 'She dived for a moment; but re-appearing, raised her right arm, and vowed that henceforth the harbour should be desolate. And,' added the old man, 'it always will be so. We have had commissions, and I know not what, about converting this place into a harbour of refuge. A harbour of refuge would be a great blessing, but not all the Government commissions in the world could keep the sand out, or make the harbour deep enough to swim a frigate, unless the parsons can find out the way to take up the merry-maid's curse.'

The Giant of the Mount

The history of the redoubtable Jack proves that St Michael's Mount was the abode of the giant Cormelian, or, as the name is sometimes given, Cormoran. We are told how Jack destroyed the giant, and the story ends. Now, the interesting part, which has been forgotten in the narrative, is not only that Cormoran lived on, but that he built the Mount, his dwelling-place. St Michael's Mount, as is tolerably well known, is an island at each rise of the tide – the distance between it and the mainland being a little more than a quarter of a mile. In the days of the giants, however, it was some six miles from the sea, and was known as The White Rock in the wood, or in Cornish, *Carreg luz en kuz*.

In this wood the giant desired to build his home, and to rear it above the trees, that he might from the top keep watch over the neighbouring country. Any person carefully observing the structure of the granite rocks will notice their tendency to a cubical form. These stones were carefully selected by the giant from the granite of the neighbouring hills, and he was for a long period employed in carrying and piling those huge masses, one on the other, in which labour he compelled his wife to aid him. It has been suggested, with much show of probability, that the confusion of the two names alluded to has arisen from the fact that the giant was called Cormoran, and that the name of his wife was Cormelian; at all events, there is no harm in adopting this hypo-thesis. The toil of lifting those granite masses from their primitive beds, and of carrying them through the forest, was excessive. It would seem that the heaviest burthens were imposed upon Cormelian, and that she was in the habit of carrying those rocky masses in her apron. At a short distance from the White Rock, which was now approaching completion, there exist large masses of greenstone rock. Cormelian saw no reason why one description of stone would not do as well as another; and one day, when the giant Cormoran was sleeping, she broke off a vast mass of the greenstone rock, and taking it in her apron, hastened towards the artificial hill with it, hoping to place it without being observed by Cormoran. When, however, Cormelian was within a short distance of the White Rock, the giant awoke, and presently perceived that his wife was, contrary to his wishes, carrying a green stone instead of a white one.

In great wrath he arose, followed her, and, with a dreadful imprecation, gave her a kick. Her apron-string broke, and the stone fell on the sand. There it has ever since remained, no human power being sufficient to remove it. The giantess died, and the mass of greenstone, resting, as it does, on clay slate rocks, became her monument. In more recent days, when the light of Christianity was dawning on the land, this famous rock was still rendered sacred: 'a little chapel' having been built on it; and to this day it is usually known as 'The Chapel Rock.'

The Lizard people

There is a tradition that the Lizard people were formerly a very inferior race. In fact it is said that they went on all fours, till the crew of a foreign vessel, wrecked on the coast, settled among them, and improved the race so much that they became as remarkable for their stature and physical development as they had been before for the reverse. At this time, as a whole, the Lizard folks certainly have among them a very large population of tall people, many of the men and women being over six feet in height.

The Padstow 'Hobby Horse'

At the time of the spring festival, which is observed at Helston as a revel in honour, probably, of Flora, and hence called the 'Furry-day,' and by the blowing of horns and gathering of the 'may' in St Ives and other places, the people of Padstow were a few years since in the habit of riding the 'hobby-horse' to water. This hobby-horse was, after it had been taken round the town, submerged in the sea.

The old people said it was once believed that this ceremony preserved the cattle of the inhabitants from disease and death. The appearance of a white horse escaping from the flood which buried the Lyonesse, is told at several points, on both the north and south coast, and the riding of the hobby-horse probably belongs to this tradition. In support of this idea, we must not forget the mermaid story associated with the harbour of Padstow.

The water-horse is a truly Celtic tradition. We have it in the Arabian Nights, and in the stories of all countries in the south of Europe. Mr Campbell in *West Highland Tales*, says he finds the horse brought prominently forward in the Breton legends, and that animal figures largely in traditions of Scotland and Ireland.

Have the miners' phrases 'a horse in the lode', applied to a mass of unproductive ground in the middle of a mineral lode, or, 'Black Jack rides a good horse,' signifying that zinc ore gives good promise for copper, anything to do with these traditions?

The Giants of Trencrom, or Trecrobben

The rough granite hill of Trecrobben rises in almost savage grandeur from the wooded lands which form the park of Trevetha, close by the picturesque village of Lelant. From the summit of this hill may be surveyed one of the most striking panoramic views in Cornwall. The country declines, rather rapidly, but still with a pleasing contour, towards the sea on the southern side. From the sandy plain, which extends from Marazion to Penzance, there stretch out two arms of land, one on the eastern side, towards the Lizard Point, and the other on the western side towards Mousehole and Lamorna, which embrace as it were that fine expanse of water known as the Mount's Bay. The most striking object, 'set in the silver sea', is the pyramidical hill St Michael's Mount, crowned with the 'castle', an unhappy mixture of church, castle, and modern dwelling-house, which, nevertheless, from its very incongruities, has a picturesque appearance when viewed from a distance. Nestling amidst the greenstone rocks, sheltered by 'the Holy Mount', is the irregular town of Marazion, or Market-Jew; and, balancing this, on the western side of 'the Green', Penzance displays her more important buildings, framed by the beautifully fertile country by which the town is surrounded.

The high lands to the westward of Penzance, with the fishing villages of Newlyn and Mousehole, the church of Paul on the summit of the hill, and the engine-house belonging to a mine at its base, have much quiet beauty under some aspects of light – the yet more western hills shutting out the Land's End from the observer's eye.

Looking from Trencrom (this is the more common name) to the south-east, the fine hills of Tregoning and Godolphin – both of which have given names to ancient Cornish families – mark the southern boundary of a district famed for its mineral wealth. Looking eastward, Carn Brea Hill, with its ancient castle and its modern monument, stands up from the tableland in rugged grandeur. This hill, 'a merry place, 'tis said, in days of yore' – when British villages were spread amidst the mighty cairns, and Cyclopean walls sheltered the inhabitants – rises to mark the most productive piece of mining-ground, of the same area, to be found in the world.

Around the towns of Camborne and Redruth are seen hundreds of miners' cottages, and scores of tall chimneys, telling of the mechanical appliances which are brought to bear upon the extraction of tin and copper from the earth. Beyond this thickly-peopled region the eye wanders yet eastwards and eventually reposes on the series of granite hills which rise beyond St Austell and stretch northward, the two highest hills in Cornwall, which are known as Roughtor and Brownwilly, being in this range.

Let the observer now turn his face northward, and a new and varied scene lies before him. Within two miles the waters of St Ives Bay break against the cliffs. On the left is the creek of Hayle, which has been fashioned by the energy of man into a useful harbour, and given rise to the foundation of two extensive iron-foundries. Between those and the sea are the hills of blown sand, which have ever been the homes of the Fairy people.

The lighthouse of Godrevy stands, a humble companion, to balance in this bay the Mount, which adorns the bay washing the southern slope of this narrow neck of land. Godrevy marks the region of sand extending to the eastward. To the north the shores become more and more rugged, culminating in St Agnes' Beacon – a hill of graceful form rising somewhat rapidly to a considerable elevation. From this the 'beetling cliffs' stretch away northward, until the bold promontory Trevose Head closes the scene, appropriately displaying another of those fine examples of humanity – a lighthouse.

To the left, towards the sea, rises the cenotaph of Knill, an eccentric man, who evidently sought to secure some immortality by this building and the silly ceremonials carried on around it, the due performance of which he has secured by bequests to the Corporation of St Ives. Around this the mining district of St Ives is seen, and her fishing-boats dotting the sea give evidence of another industry of vast importance to the town and neighbourhood. Westward of St Ives, hills more brown and rugged than any which have yet been viewed stretch away to Zennor, Morva, and St Just, and these, girding the scene beneath our feet, shut out from us the region of the Land's End.

On the summit of this hill, which is only surpassed in savage grandeur by Carn Brea, the giants built a castle – the four entrances to which still remain in Cyclopean massiveness to attest the Herculean powers by which such mighty blocks were piled upon each other. There the giant chieftains dwelt in awful state. Along the serpentine road, passing up the hill to the principal gateway, they dragged their captives, and on the great flat rocks within the castle they sacrificed them. Almost every rock still bears some name connected with the giants – 'a race may perish, but the name endures'. The treasures of the giants who dwell here are said to have been buried in the days of their troubles when they were perishing before the conquerors of their land. Their gold and jewels were hidden deep in the granite caves of this hill, and secured by spells as potent as those which Merlin placed upon his hoarded treasures. They are securely preserved even to the present day, and carefully guarded from man by the Spriggans, or Trolls.

The Fairy Fair in Germoe

Bal Lane in Germoe was a notorious place for piskies. One night Daniel Champion and his comrade came to Godolphin Bridge; they were a little bit 'overtook' with liquor. They said that when they came to Bal Lane, they found it covered all over from end to end, and the Small People holding a fair there with all sorts of merchandise – the prettiest sight they ever met with. Champion was sure he saw his child there; for a few nights before, his child in the evening was as beautiful a one as could be seen anywhere, but in the morning was changed for one as ugly and wizened as could be; and he was sure the Small People had done it. Next day, telling the story at Croft Gothal, his comrade was knocked backward, thrown into the bob-pit, and just killed. Obliged to be carried to his home, Champion followed and was telling of their adventure with the Small People, when one said, 'Don't speak about them; they're wicked, spiteful devils.' No sooner were the words uttered than the speaker was thrown clean over stairs and bruised dreadfully – a convincing proof to all present of the reality of the existence of the Small Folks.

The rival giants

Those have visited the Logan Rock will be familiar with the several groups which form the Treryn promontory. Treryn Castle, an ancient British fortress, the Cyclopean walls of which, and its outer earthwork, can still be traced, was the dwelling of a famous giant and his wife. I have heard it said that he gave his name to this place, but that is, of course, doubtful. This giant was chief of a numerous band, and by his daring he held possession, against the giants of the Mount, of all the lands west of Penzance. Amongst the hosts who owed allegiance to him was a remarkable fine young fellow, who had his abode in a cave, in the pile of rocks upon which the Logan Rock stands. This young giant grew too fond of the giantess, and it would appear that the lady was not unfavourably inclined towards him. Of their love passes, however, we know nothing. Tradition has only told us that the giantess was one day reclining on the rock still known as the Giant Lady's Chair, while the good old giant was dosing in the Giant's Chair which stands near it, when the young and wicked lover stole behind his chief and stabbed him in the belly with a knife. The giant fell over the rocks to the level ridge below, and there he lay, rapidly pouring out his life-blood. From this spot the young murderer kicked him into the sea, ere yet his life was quite extinct, and he perished in the waters.

The guilty pair took possession of Treryn Castle, and, we are told, lived happily for many years.

The mutton feast

An old tradition – the particulars of which I have failed to recover – says that a flock of sheep were blown from the Gwithian Sands over into St Ives Bay, and that the St Ives fishermen caught them, believing them to be a new variety of fish, either in their nets, or with hook and line, and brought them ashore as their night's catch.

Jago's demon

The vicar of Wendron, who bore the name of Jago, appears to have had strange intercourse with the invisible world; or, rather, the primitive people of this district believe him to have possessed supernatural powers. Any one visiting the parish of Wendron will be struck with many distinguishing features in its inhabitants. It would appear as if a strange people had settled down amidst the races already inhabiting the spot, and that they had studiously avoided any intimate connection with their neighbours. The dialect of the Wendron people is unlike any other in Cornwall, and there are many customs existing amongst them which are not found in any other part of the county.

Until of late years, the inhabitants of Wendron were quite uneducated – hence the readiness with which they associate ancient superstitions with comparatively modern individuals.

The Reverend Mr Jago was no doubt a man who impressed this people with the powers of his knowledge. Hence we are told that no spirit walking the earth could resist the spells laid upon him by Jago. By his prayers – or powers – many a night wanderer has been put back into his grave, and so confined that the poor ghost could never again get loose. To the evil-disposed, Mr Jago was a terror. All Wendron believed that every act was visible to the parson at the moment it was done – day or night it mattered not. He has been known to pick a thief at once out of a crowd, and criminal men or women could not endure the glance of his eye. Many a person has at once confessed to guilty deeds of which they have been suspected the moment they have been brought before Mr Jago.

We are told that he had spirits continually waiting upon him, though invisible until he desired them to appear. The parson rode far and wide over the moorland of his parish. He never took a groom with him; for, the moment he alighted from his horse, he had only to strike the earth with his whip, and up came a demon-groom to take charge of the steed.

The phantom ship

Years long ago, one night, a gig's crew was called to go off to a 'hobble', to the westwards of St Ives Head. No sooner was one boat launched than several others were put off from the shore, and a stiff chase was maintained, each one being eager to get to the ship, as she had the appearance of a foreign trader. The hull was clearly visible: she was a schooner-rigged vessel, with a light over her bows.

Away they pulled, and the boat which had been first launched still kept ahead by dint of mechanical power and skill. All the men had thrown off their jackets to row with more freedom. At length the helmsman cried out, 'Stand ready to board her.' The sailor rowing the bow oar slipped it out of the row-lock, and stood on the forethought, taking his jacket on his arm, ready to spring aboard.

The vessel came so close to the boat that they could see the men, and the bow-oar man made a grasp at her bulwarks. His hand found nothing solid, and he fell, being caught by one of his mates, back into the boat, instead of into the water. Then ship and lights disappeared. The next morning the *Neptune* of London, Captain Richard Grant, was wrecked at Gwithian, and all perished. The captain's body was picked up after a few days, and that of his son also. They were both buried in Gwithian churchyard.

The giants at play

In Cornwall there are evidences that these Titans were a sportive race. Huge rocks are preserved to show where they played at trap-ball, at hurling, and other athletic games. The giants of Trecrobben and St Michael's Mount often met for a game at bob-buttons. The Mount was the 'bob,' on which flat masses of granite were placed to serve as buttons, and Trecrobben Hill was the 'mit', or the spot from which the throw was made. This order was sometimes reversed. On the outside of St Michael's Mount, many a granite slab which had been knocked off the 'bob' is yet to be found; and numerous piles of rough cubical masses of the same rock, said to be the granite of Trecrobben Hill, show how eagerly the game was played.

Trecrobben Hill was well chosen by the giants as the site of their castle. From it they surveyed the country on every side; and friend or enemy was seen at a considerable distance as he approached the guarded spot. It is as clear as tradition can make it, that Trecrobben was the centre of a region full of giants. On Lescudjack Hill, close to Penzance, there is 'The Giant's Round,' evidently the scene of many a sanguinary conflict, since the Cornish antiquarian authority Borlase informs us, that Lesgudzhek signifies the 'Castle of the Bloody Field'. On the cairn at Gulval are several impressions on the rocks, all referable to the giants. In Madron there is the celebrated 'Giant's Cave'; and the well known Lanyon cromlech is reported by some to be the 'Giant's Coit,' while others declare it to be the 'Giant's Table'. Cairn Galva, again, is celebrated for its giant; and, indeed, every hill within sight has some monument preserving the memory of 'the Titans fierce'.

The witch and the toad

An old woman called Alsey – usually Aunt Alsey – occupied a small cottage in Anthony, one of a row which belonged to a tradesman living in Dock – as Devonport was then designated, to distinguish it from Plymouth. The old woman possessed a very violent temper, and this, more than anything else, fixed upon her the character of being a witch.

Her landlord had frequently sought his rent, and just as frequently he received nothing but abuse. He had, on the occasion to which our narrative refers, crossed the Tamar and walked to Anthony, with the firm resolve of securing his rent, now long in arrear, and of turning the old termagant out of the cottage. A violent scene ensued, and the vicious old woman, more than a match for a really kind-hearted and quiet man, remained the mistress of the situation. She seated herself in the door of her cottage and cursed her landlord's wife, 'the child she was carrying', and all belonging to him, with so devilish a spite that Mr — owned he was fairly driven away in terror.

On returning home, he, of course, told his wife all the circumstances; and while they were discoursing on the subject – the whole story being attentively listened to by their daughter, then a young girl, who is now my informant – a woman came into the shop requiring some articles which they sold. 'Sit still, father,' said Mrs — to her husband; 'you must be tired. I will see to the shop.' So she went from the parlour into the shop, and, hearing the wants of her customer, proceeded to supply them; gossiping gaily, as was her wont, to interest the buyer. Mrs — was weighing one of the articles required when something falling heavily from the ceiling of the shop struck the beam out of her hand, and both – the falling body and scales – came together with much noise on to the counter. At the same instant both women screamed, the shopkeeper calling also 'Father! father!' – meaning her husband thereby – with great energy.

Mr — and his daughter were in the shop instantly, and there, on the counter, they saw an enormous and most ugly toad sprawling amidst the chains of the scales. The first action of the man was to turn back to the parlour, seize the tongs, and return to the shop. He grasped the swollen toad with the tongs, the vicious creature spitting all the time, and, without a word, he went back and flung it behind the block of wood which was burning in the grate. The object of terror being removed, the wife, who was shortly to become the mother of another child, though usually a woman who had great command over her feelings, fainted.

This circumstance demanding all their attention, the toad was forgotten. The shock was a severe one; and although Mrs — was restored in a little time to her senses, she again and again became faint. Those fits continuing, her medical attendant, Dr — was sent for, and on his arrival he ordered that his patient should be immediately placed in bed, and the husband was informed that he must be prepared for a premature birth.

The anxiety occasioned by these circumstances, and the desire to afford every relief to his wife, so fully occupied Mr —, that for an hour or two he entirely forgot the cause of all this mischief; or, perhaps satisfying himself that the toad was burnt to ashes, he had no curiosity to look after it. He was, however, suddenly summoned from the bedroom, in which he was with his wife, by his daughter calling to him, in a voice of terror:

'O Father, the toad, the toad!'
Mr — rushed downstairs, and he then discovered that the toad, though severely burnt, had escaped destruction. It must have crawled up

over the log of wood, and from it have fallen down amongst the ashes. There it was now making useless struggles to escape, by climbing over the fender.

The tongs were again put in requisition, with the intention this time of carrying the reptile out of the house. Before, however, he had time to do so, a man from Anthony came hastily into the shop with the information that Aunt Alsey had fallen into the fire, as the people supposed, in a fit, and that she was nearly burnt to death. This man had been sent off with two commissions – one to fetch the doctor, and the other to bring Mr — with him, as much of the cottage had been injured by fire, communicated to it by the old woman's dress.

In as short a time as possible the parish surgeon and Mr — were at Anthony and too truly they found the old woman most severely burnt – so seriously, indeed, there was no chance that one so aged could rally from the shock which her system must have received. However, a litter was carefully prepared, the old woman was placed in it, and carried to the workhouse. Every attention was given to her situation, but she never recovered perfect consciousness, and during the night she died.

The toad, which we left inside the fender in front of a blazing fire, was removed from a position so trying to any cold-blooded animal, by the servant, and thrown, with a 'hugh' and a shudder, upon one of the flower-beds in the small garden behind the house.

There it lay the next morning, dead, and when examined by Mr —, it was found that all the injuries sustained by the toad corresponded with those received by the poor old wretch, who had no doubt fallen a victim to passion.

As we have only to deal with the mysterious relation which existed between the witch and the toad, it is not necessary that we should attend further to the innocent victim of an old woman's vengeance, than to say that eventually a babe was born – that that babe grew to be a handsome man, was an officer in the navy, and having married, went to sea, and perished, leaving a widow with an unborn child to lament his loss. Whether this was a result of the witch's curse, those who are more deeply skilled in witchcraft than I am may perhaps tell.

The giant Bolster

This mighty man held especial possession of the hill formerly known as Carne Bury-anacht or Bury-allack, 'the sparstone grave,' and sometimes called 'St Agnes' Ball' and 'St Agnes' Pestis', but which is now named, from the use made of the hill during the long war, St Agnes' Beacon. He has left his name to a very interesting, and undoubtedly most ancient earthwork, which still exists at the base of the hill, and evidently extended from Trevaunance Porth as far as Chapel Porth, enclosing the most important tin district in St Agnes. This is constantly called 'The Bolster'.

Bolster must have been of enormous size; since it is stated that he could stand with one foot on St Agnes' Beacon and the other on Carn Brea; these hills being distant, as the bird flies, six miles, his immensity will be clear to all. In proof of this, there still exists, in the valley running upwards from Chapel Porth, a stone in which may yet be seen the impression of the giant's fingers. On one occasion, Bolster, when enjoying his usual stride from the Beacon to Carn Brea, felt thirsty, and stooped to drink out of the well at Chapel Porth, resting, while he did so, on the stone.

We hear but little of the wives of our giants; but Bolster had a wife, who was made to labour hard by her tyrannical husband. On the top of St Agnes' Beacon there yet exist the evidences of the useless labours to which this unfortunate giantess was doomed, in grouped masses of small stones. These, it is said, have all been gathered from an estate at the foot of the hill, immediately adjoining the village of St Agnes. This farm is to the present day remarkable for its freedom from stones, though situated amidst several others, which, like most lands reclaimed from the moors of this district, have stones in abundance mixed with the soil. Whenever Bolster was angry with his wife, he compelled her to pick stones, and to carry them in her apron to the top of the hill.

There is some confusion in the history of this giant, and of the blessed St Agnes to whom the church is dedicated. They are supposed to have lived at the same time, which, according to our views, is scarcely probable, believing, as we do, that no giants existed long after their defeat at Plymouth by Brutus and Corineus. There may have been an earlier saint of the same name; or may not Saint Enns or Anns, the popular name of this parish, indicate some other lady?

Be this as it may, the giant Bolster became deeply in love with St Agnes, who is reputed to have been singularly beautiful, and a pattern woman of virtue. The giant allowed the lady no repose. He followed her incessantly, proclaiming his love, and filling the air with the tempests of his sighs and groans. St Agnes lectured Bolster in vain on the impropriety of his conduct, he being already a married man. This availed not; her prayers to him to relieve her from his importunities were also in vain. The persecuted lady finding there was no release for her, while this monster existed, resolved to be rid of him at any cost, and eventually succeeded by the following stratagem: Agnes appeared at length to be persuaded of the intensity of the giant's love, but she told him she required yet one small proof more. There exists at Chapel Porth a hole in the cliff at the termination of the valley. If Bolster would fill this hole with his blood the lady would no longer look coldly on him.

This huge bestrider-of-the-hills thought that it was an easy thing which was required of him, and felt that he could fill many such holes and be none the weaker for the loss of blood. Consequently, stretching his great arm across the hole, he plunged a knife into a vein, and a torrent of gore issued forth. Roaring and seething the blood fell to the bottom, and the giant expected in a few minutes to see the test of his devotion made evident, in the filling of the hole. It required much more blood than Bolster had supposed; still it must in a short time be filled, so he bled on. Hour after hour the blood flowed from the vein, yet the hole was not filled. Eventually the giant fainted from exhaustion. The strength of life within his mighty frame enabled him to rally, yet he had no power to lift himself from the ground, and he was unable to stanch the wound which he had made. Thus it was, that after many throes, the giant Bolster died!

The cunning saint, in proposing this task to Bolster, was well aware that the hole opened at the bottom into the sea, and that as rapidly as the blood flowed into the hole it ran from it, and did

The multitudinous seas incarnadine,
Making the green one red.

Thus the lady got rid of her hated lover; Mrs Bolster was released, and the district freed from the presence of a tyrant. The hole at Chapel Porth still retains the evidences of the truth of this tradition, in the red stain which marks the track down which flowed the giant's blood.

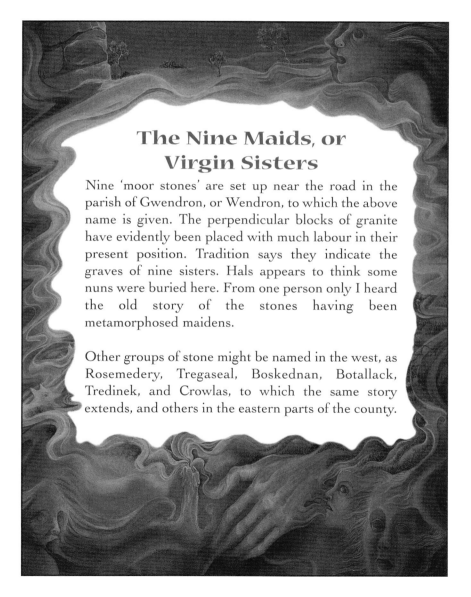

The Nine Maids, or Virgin Sisters

Nine 'moor stones' are set up near the road in the parish of Gwendron, or Wendron, to which the above name is given. The perpendicular blocks of granite have evidently been placed with much labour in their present position. Tradition says they indicate the graves of nine sisters. Hals appears to think some nuns were buried here. From one person only I heard the old story of the stones having been metamorphosed maidens.

Other groups of stone might be named in the west, as Rosemedery, Tregaseal, Boskednan, Botallack, Tredinek, and Crowlas, to which the same story extends, and others in the eastern parts of the county.

Kenidzhek witch

On the tract called the 'Gump' near Kenidzhek is a beautiful well of clear water, not far from which was a miner's cot, in which dwelt two miners with their sister. They told her never to go to the well after dark; they would fetch the water for her. However, on one Saturday night she had forgotten to get in a supply for the morrow, so she went off to the well. Passing by a gap in a broken-down hedge (called a gurgo) near the well, she saw an old woman sitting down, wrapped in a red shawl; she asked her what she did there at that time of night, but received no reply; she thought this rather strange, but plunged her pitcher in the well. When she drew it up, though a perfectly sound vessel, it contained no water; she tried again and again, and though she saw the water rushing in at the mouth of the pitcher, it was sure to be empty when lifted out. She then became rather frightened, spoke again to the old woman, but receiving no answer, hastened away, and came in great alarm to her brothers. They told her that it was on account of this old woman they did not wish her to go to the well at night. What she saw was the ghost of old Moll, a witch who had been a great terror to the people in her lifetime, and had laid many fearful spells on them. They said they saw her sitting in the gap by the wall every night when going to bed.

The legend of Tamara

The lovely nymph Tamara was born in a cavern. Although her parents were spirits of the earth, the child loved the light of day. Often had they chided her for yielding to her desires and visiting the upper world; and often had they warned her against the consequences which would probably arise from her neglect of their advice. The giants of the moors were to be feared; and it was from these that the earth spirits desired to protect their child.

Tamara – beautiful, young, heedless – never lost an opportunity of looking on the glorious sun. Two sons of Dartmoor giants – Tavy and Tawrage – had seen the fair maid, and longed to possess her. Long was their toil, and the wild maiden often led them over mountain and moor in playful chase.

Under a bush in Morewinstow, one day, both Tavy and Tawrage came upon Tamara. They resolved now to compel her to declare upon which of them her choice should fall. The young men used every persuasion, and called her by every endearing name. Her parents had missed Tamara, and they sought and found her seated between the sons of the giants whom they hated. The gnome father caused a deep sleep to fall on the eye of Tavy and Tawrage, and then he endeavoured to persuade his daughter to return to his subterranean cell.

Tamara would not leave her lovers. In his rage, the gnome cursed his daughter and, by the might of his curse, changed her into a river, which should flow on for ever to the salt sea. The lovely Tamara dissolved in tears, and as a crystal stream of exceeding beauty the waters glided onward to the ocean.

At length Tavy awoke. His Tamara was gone; he fled to his father in the hills. The giant knew of the metamorphosis, and, to ease the anguish of his son, he transformed him into a stream. Rushing over rocks, running through morasses, gliding along valleys, and murmuring amidst the groves, Tavy still goes on seeking for Tamara – his only joy being that he runs by her side and that, mingling their waters, they glide together to the eternal sea.

Tawrage awakened after a long sleep. He divined what had taken place, and fled to the hills to an enchanter. At his prayer he, too, was changed to a stream; but he mistook the road along which Tamara had gone, and onward, ever sorrowing, he flows away-away-away from his Tamara for ever. Thus originated the Tamar, the Tavy, and the Taw.

The fairy miners – the knockers

At Ransom Mine the Knockers were always very active in their subterranean operations. In every part of the mine their knockings were heard, but most especially were they busy in one particular 'end'. There was a general impression that great wealth must exist at this part of the lode. Yet, notwithstanding that inducements of very high 'tribute' were held out to the miners, no pair of men could be found brave enough to venture on the ground of the 'Bockles'.

An old man and his son, called Trenwith, who lived near Bosprenis, went out one midsummer eve, about midnight, and watched until they saw the 'Smae People' bringing up the shining ore. It is said they were possessed of some secret by which they could communicate with the fairy people. Be this as it may, they told the little miners that they would save them all the trouble of breaking down the ore, that they would bring 'to grass' for them, one-tenth of the 'richest stuff' and leave it properly dressed, if they would quietly give them up this end. An agreement of some kind was come to. The old man and his son took the 'pitch', and in a short time realised much wealth. The old man never failed to keep to his bargain, and leave the tenth of the ore for his friends. He died. The son was avaricious and selfish. He sought to cheat the Knockers, but he ruined himself by so doing. The 'lode' failed; nothing answered with him; disappointed, he took to drink, squandered all the money his father had made, and died a beggar.

The great Wrath or Ralph

Not far from Portreath there exists a remarkable fissure, or gorge, on the coast, formed by the wearing out, through the action of the sea, of a channel of ground softer than that which exists on either side of it. This is generally known as Ralph's Cupboard; and one tale is that Ralph was a famous smuggler, who would run his little vessel, even in dark nights, into the shelter afforded by this gorge, and safely land his goods. Another is, that it was formerly a cavern in which dwelt Wrath – a huge giant, who was the terror of the fishermen. Sailing from St Ives, they ever avoided the Cupboard; as they said, 'Nothing ever came out of it which was unfortunate enough to get into it.' Wrath is reputed to have watched for those who were drifted towards his Cupboard by currents, or driven in by storms. It is said that wading out to sea, he tied the boats to his girdle, and quietly walked back to his den, making, of course, all the fishermen his prey. The roof of the cavern is supposed to have fallen in after the death of the giant, leaving the open chasm as we now see it.

Morva or Morveth

The parish of this name is situated on the north-west coast of Cornwall, the parish of St Just being on its western borders, and that of Zennor on the east, between it and St Ives. The Cornish historian Tonkin says, 'Morva signifies *Locus Maritimus*, a place near the sea, as this parish is. The name is sometimes written Morveth, implying much the same sense.'

The similarity of this name to 'Morgan,' sea-women, and 'Morverch,' sea-daughters, which Mr Keightley has shown us is applied to the mermaids of the Breton ballads, is not a little curious. There are several stories current in this parish of ladies seen on the rocks, of ladies going off from the shore to peculiar isolated rocks at special seasons, and of ladies sitting weeping and wailing on the shore.

Mr Blight, in his *Week at the Land's End*, speaking of the church in the adjoining parish of Zennor, which still remains in nearly its primitive condition whereas Morva church is a modern structure, says: 'Some of the bench ends were carved; on one is a strange figure of a mermaid, which to many might seem out of character in a church.' (Mr Blight gives a drawing of this bench end.) This is followed by a quotation bearing the initials R.S.H., which, it is presumed, are those of the Rev. R.S.Hawker, of Morwenstow:

The fishermen who were the ancestors of the Church, came from the Galilean waters to haul for men. We, born to God at the font, are children of the water. Therefore, all the early symbolism of the Church was of and from the sea. The carvure of the early arches was taken from the sea and its creatures. Fish, dolphins, mermen, and mermaids abound in the early types, transferred to wood and stone.

Surely the poet of 'the Western Shore' might have explained the fact of the figures of mermaids being carved on the bench ends of some of the old churches with less difficulty, had he remembered that nearly all the churches on the coast of Cornwall were built by and for fishermen, to whom the superstitions of mermen and mermaidens had the familiarity of a creed.

The intimate connection between the inhabitants of Brittany, of Cornwall, and of Wales, would appear to lead to the conclusion that the Breton word morverch, or mermaid, had much to do with the name of this parish, Morva, of Morvel, near Liskeard, and probably of Morwenstow, of which the vicar, Mr Hawker, writes:

'My glebe occupies a position of wild and singular beauty. Its western boundary is the sea, skirted by tall and tremendous cliffs, and near their brink, with the exquisite taste of ecclesiastical antiquity, is placed the church. The original and proper designation of the parish is Morwenstow – that is, Morwenna's Stow, or station; but it has been corrupted by recent usage, like many other local names.'

The devil's doorway

In the slate (killas) formations behind Polperro is a good example of a fault. The geologist, in the pride of his knowledge, refers this to some movement of the solid mass – a rending of the rocks, produced either by the action of some subterranean force lifting the earth-crust, or by a depression of one division of the rocks. The wisdom of our grandfathers led them to a conclusion widely different from this.

The mighty ruler of the realms of darkness, who is known to have an especial fondness for rides at midnight, 'to see how his little ones thrive,' ascending from his subterranean country, chose this spot as his point of egress.

As he rose from below in his fiery car, drawn by a gigantic jet black steed, the rocks gave way before him, and the rent at Polperro remains to this day to convince all unbelievers. Not only this, as his Satanic majesty burst through the slate rocks, his horse, delighted with the airs of this upper world, reared in wild triumph, and, planting again his hoof upon the ground, made these islands shake as with an earthquake; and he left the deep impression of his burning foot behind. There, any unbeliever may see the hoof-shaped pool, unmistakable evidence of the wisdom of the days gone by.

The witches of the Logan Stone

Who that has travelled into Cornwall but has visited the Logan Stone? Numerous logan rocks exist on the granite hills of the county, but that remarkable mass which is poised on the cubical masses forming its Cyclopean support, at Trereen, is beyond all others the Logan Stone.

A more sublime spot could not have been chosen by the Bardic priesthood for any ordeal connected with their worship; and even admitting that nature may have disposed the huge mass to wear away, so as to rest delicately poised on a pivot, it is highly probable that the wild worship of the untrained tribes, who had passed to these islands from the shores of the Mediterranean Sea, may have led them to believe that some superhuman power belonged to such a strangely-balanced mass of rock.

Nothing can be more certain than that through all time, passing on from father to son, there has been a wild reverence of this mass of rock; and long after the days when the Druid ceased to be there is every reason for believing that the Christian priests, if they did not encourage, did not forbid the use of this and similar rocks to be used as places of ordeal by the uneducated and superstitious people around.

Hence the mass of rock on which is poised the Logan Stone has ever been connected with the supernatural. To the south of the Logan Rock is a high peak of granite, towering above the other rocks; this is known as the Castle Peak.

No one can say for how long a period, but most certainly for ages, this peak has been the midnight rendezvous for witches. Many a man, and woman too, now sleeping quietly in the churchyard of St Levan, would, had they the power, attest to have seen the witches flying into the Castle

Peak on moonlit nights, mounted on the stems of the ragwort and bringing with them the things necessary to make their charms potent and strong.

This place was long noted as the gathering place of the army of witches who took their departure for Wales, where they would luxuriate at the most favoured seasons of the year upon the milk of the Welshmen's cows. From this peak many a struggling ship has been watched by a malignant crone, while she has been brewing the tempest to destroy it; and many a rejoicing chorus has been echoed, in horror, by the cliffs around, when the witches have been croaking their miserable delight over the perishing crews, as they have watched man, woman and child drowning, whom they were presently to rob of the treasures they were bringing home from other lands.

Upon the rocks behind the Logan Rock it would appear that every kind of mischief which can befall man or beast was once brewed by the St Levan witches.

The spectre ship of Porthcurno

Porthcurno Cove is situated a little to the west of the Logan Stone. There, as in nearly all the coves around the coast, there once existed a small chapel or oratory, which appears to have been dedicated to St Leven. There exists now a little square enclosure about the size of a sheep's house, which is all that remains of this holy place. Looking up the valley, you may see a few trees, with the chimney tops and part of the roof of an old-fashioned house. That place is Raftra, where they say St Leven church was to have been built; but as fast as the stones were taken there by day, they were removed by night to the place of the present church. (These performances are usually the act of the devil, but I have no information as to the saint or sinner who did this work.) Raftra House, at the time it was built, was the largest mansion west of Penzance. It is said to have been erected by the Tresillians, and, ere it was finished, they were obliged to sell house and lands for less than it had cost them to build the house.

This valley is, in every respect, a melancholy spot, and during a period of storms or at night it is exactly the place which might well be haunted by demon revellers. In the days of the saint from whom the parish has its name, St Leven, he lived a long way from the cove, at a place called Bodelan, and his influence made that, which is now so dreary, a garden. By his pure holiness he made the wilderness a garden of flowers, and spread gladness where now is desolation. Few persons cared to cross that valley after nightfall; and it is not more than thirty years since that I had a narrative from an inhabitant of Penberth, that he himself had seen the spectre ship sailing over the land.

This strange apparition is said to have been observed frequently, coming in from sea about nightfall, when the mists were rising from the marshy ground in the Bottoms.

Onward came the ill-omened craft. It passed steadily through the breakers on the shore, glided up over the sands, and steadily pursued its course over the dry land, as if it had been water. She is described to have been a black, square-rigged, single-masted affair, usually, but not always, followed by a boat. No crew was ever seen. It is supposed they were below, and that the hatches were battened down. On it went to Bodelan, where St Leven formerly dwelt. It would then steer its course to Chygwiden, and there vanish like smoke.

Many of the old people have seen this ship, and no one ever saw it, upon whom some bad luck was not sure to fall.

This ship is somehow connected with a strange man who returned from sea, and went to live at Chygwiden. It may be five hundred years since, it may be but fifty.

He was accompanied by a servant of foreign and forbidding aspect, who continued to be his only attendant, and this servant was never known to speak to any one save his master. It is said by some that they were pirates; others make them more familiar, by calling them privateers; while some insist upon it they were American buccaneers. Whatever they may have been, there was but little seen of them by any of their neighbours. They kept a boat at Porthcurno Cove, and at daylight they would start for sea, never returning until night, and not infrequently remaining out the whole of the night, especially if the weather was tempestuous. This kind of sea-life was varied by hunting. It mattered not to them whether it was day or night; when the storm was loudest, there was this strange man, accompanied either by his servant or by the devil, and the midnight cry of his dogs would disturb the country.

This mysterious being died, and then the servant sought the aid of a few of the peasantry to bear his coffin to the churchyard. The corpse was laid in the grave, around which the dogs were gathered, with the foreigner in their midst. As soon as the earth was thrown on the coffin, man and dogs disappeared, and, strange to say, the boat disappeared at the same moment from the cove. It has never since been seen; and from that day to this, no one has been able to keep a boat in Porthcurno Cove.

The cock-crow stone

A rock of white marble (?) with many rock basins on its surface lies in Looe harbour, under Saunder's Lane, and is now covered by every tide. This stone once stood on the top of an elevated rock near it, and when in this position, whenever it heard a cock crow in the neighbouring farmyard of Hay, it turned round three times.

The topmost stone of that curious pile of rocks in the parish of St Cleer known as the Cheesewring is gifted in like manner.

The Garrack Zans

A few years – really but a few years – since, the stone altars on which the first inhabitants of these islands lit their holy fires had yet a place amongst us. In the village of Roskestall stood one such altar; in Treen was to be found another. These huge masses of rock, rendered sacred by the memories surrounding them, have been wantonly removed, and employed in most cases in furnishing pillars at the 'grand entrances' of the houses of the squire farmers of the Land's End district; or they have been yet more rudely served, and are to be found at the entrance to a pigsty, or in the gate-posts to a potato-field.

The extinction of several of the old families is, to the present day, ascribed by the peasantry to the unholy act of removing or breaking up of the Garrick Zans in the village of Escols. The rock in the village of Mayon was called indifferently table-mayon (men), or the Garrack Zans. Within our memory is the gathering of the villagers around the Holy Rock. It was their custom, when anything was stolen, or a misdemeanour committed, to light a fire on this altar, and when the fagots were in full blaze, all those who sought to prove their innocence took a burning stick from the rock and spat on the blazing end. If they could extinguish the fire by spitting on the stick, they were declared innocent; but if their mouth was so dry as not to generate sufficient moisture to be heard 'frizzing' on it, that unfortunate individual was suspected, if not declared, to be guilty.

The Midsummer bonfire was first lighted on the rock in Escols, next on the Chapel Hill; then all the other beacon hills were soon ablaze. Many superstitious rites were formerly performed on the Garrack Zans, which are only found now as the amusements of young people on the eves of St Agnes and Midsummer.

Peter the Devil

The church at Altarnun is said to have been built from the remains of an ancient nunnery which had been founded in the early days of Christianity by the saint to whom it was dedicated.

There was a peculiar sanctity about all that surrounded this little church and its holy well, and few were unfaithful enough to scoff at any of the holy traditions of the sacred place.

About the time of Charles II, an under-clerk or deacon of this church was called Peter, and he is said to have been a man of exceedingly bad character. He scoffed at holy things, and – unless he was belied – he made use of his position for merely temporal benefit, and was not remarkable for his honesty. He was, moreover, the terror of the neighbourhood. Common report insisting on it that Peter had been known to disentomb the dead, whether for the purpose of stealing rings and other trinkets which may have been buried, as some said, or for the purpose of renewing his youth, as others suggested, by mysterious contact with the dead, was not clearly made out. He was invariably called Peter Jowle, or Joule – that is, Peter the Devil. At the age of a hundred he was a gray-headed, toothless man; but then, by some diabolical incantation, he is said to have caused new black hairs to spring forth amongst those which were white with age, and then also new teeth grew in his jaws. Peter is said to have died when he was more than a hundred and fifty years old.

Christmas Eve in the mines

On Christmas Eve, in former days, the small people, or the spriggans, would meet at the bottom of the deepest mines, and have a midnight mass. Then those who were in the mine would hear voices, melodious beyond all earthly voices, singing, 'Now well! now well'; and the strains of some deep-toned organ would shake the rocks.

Of the grandeur of those meetings, old stories could not find words sufficiently sonorous to speak; it was therefore left to the imagination.

But this was certain, the temple formed by the fairy bands in which to celebrate the eve of the birth of a Saviour, in whose mercy they all had hope, was of the most magnificent description.

Midsummer-eve and New-year's day and eve are holidays with the miners. It has been said they refuse to work on those days from superstitious reasons. I never heard of any.

How Pengerswick became a sorcerer

The first Pengerswick, by whom the castle, which still bears his name, was built, was a proud man, and desired to ally himself with some of the best families of Cornwall. He wished his son to wed a lady who was very much older than himself, who is said to have been connected with the Godolphin family. This elderly maiden had a violent desire either for the young man or the castle – it is not very clear which. The young Pengerswick gave her no return for the manifestations of love which she lavished upon him. Eventually, finding that all her attempts to win the young man's love were abortive, and that all the love potions brewed for her by the Witch of Fraddam were of no avail, she married the old lord – mainly, it is said, to be revenged on the son.

The witch had a niece who, though poor, possessed considerable beauty; she was called Bitha. This young girl was frequently employed by her aunt and the lady of Godolphin to aid them in their spells on the young Pengerswick, and, as a natural consequence, she fell desperately in love with him herself. Bitha ingratiated herself with the lady of Pengerswick, now the stepmother of the young man, and was selected as her maid. This gave her many opportunities of seeing and speaking to young Pengerswick, and her passion increased. The old stepdame was still passionately fond of the young man, and never let a chance escape her which she thought likely to lead to the excitement of passion in his heart towards her. In all her attempts she failed. Her love was turned to hate; and having seen her stepson in company with Bitha, this hate was quickened by the more violent jealousy. Every means which her wicked mind could devise were employed to destroy the young man. Bitha had learned from her aunt, the Witch of Fraddam, much of her art, and she devoted herself to counteract the spells of her mistress.

The stepmother failing to accomplish her ends, resolved to ruin young Pengerswick with his father. She persuaded the old man that his son really entertained a violent passion for her, and that she was compelled to confine herself to her tower in fear. The aged woman prevailed on Lord Pengerswick to hire a gang of outlandish sailors to carry his son away and sell him for a slave, giving him to believe that she should herself in a short time present him with an heir.

The young Pengerswick escaped all their plots, and at his own good time he disappeared from the castle, and for a long period was never heard of.

The mistress and maid plotted and counter-plotted to secure the old Pengerswick's wealth; and when he was on his death-bed, Bitha informed him of the vile practices of his wife, and consoled him with the information that he was dying from the effects of poison given him by her.

The young lord, after long years, returned from some Eastern lands with a princess for his wife, learned in all the magic sciences of those enchanted lands. He found his stepmother shut up in her chamber, with her skin covered with scales like a serpent, from the effects of the poisons which she had so often been distilling for the old lord and his son. She refused to be seen, and eventually cast herself into the sea, to the relief of all parties.

Bitha fared not much better. She lived on the Downs in St Hilary; and from the poisonous fumes she had inhaled, and from her dealings with the devil, her skin became the colour of that of a toad.

The pirate wrecker and the death ship

One lovely evening in the autumn, a strange ship was seen at a short distance from Cape Cornwall. The little wind there was blew from the land, but she did not avail herself of it. She was evidently permitted to drift with the tide, which was flowing southward and curving in round Whitesand Bay towards the Land's-End. The vessel, from her peculiar rig, created no small amount of alarm amongst the fishermen, since it told them that she was manned by pirates; and a large body of men and women watched her movements from behind the rocks at Caraglose. At length, when within a couple of pistol-shots off the shore, a boat was lowered and manned. Then a man, whose limited movements showed him to be heavily ironed, was brought to the side of the ship and evidently forced – for several pistols were held at his head – into the boat, which then rowed rapidly to the shore in Priest's Cove. The waves of the Atlantic Ocean fell so gently on the strand, that there was no difficulty in beaching the boat. The prisoner was made to stand up, and his ponderous chains were removed from his arms and ankles. In a frenzy of passion he attacked the sailors, but they were too many and too strong for him, and the fight terminated by his being thrown into the water, and left to scramble up on the dry sands. They pushed the boat off with a wild shout, and this man stood uttering fearful imprecations on his former comrades.

It subsequently became known that this man was so monstrously wicked that even the pirates would no longer endure him, and hence they had recourse to this means of ridding themselves of him.

It is not necessary to tell how this wretch settled himself at Tregaseal, and lived by a system of wrecking, pursued with unheard-of cruelties and cunning. 'It's too frightful to tell,' says my correspondent, 'what was said about his doings. We scarcely believed half of the vile things we heard, till we saw what took place at his death. But one can't say he died, because he was taken off bodily. We shall never know the scores, perhaps hundreds of ships that old sinner has brought on the cliffs, by fastening his lantern to the neck of his horse, with its head tied close to the forefoot. The horse, when driven along the cliff, would, by its motion, cause the lantern to be taken for the stemlight of a ship; then the vessel would come right in on the rocks, since those on board would expect to find plenty of sea-room and, if any of the poor sailors escaped a watery grave, the old wretch would give them a worse death, by knocking them on the head with his hatchet, or cutting off their hands as they tried to grasp the ledges of the rocks.

A life of extreme wickedness was at length closed with circumstances of unusual terror – so terrible, that the story is told with feelings of awe even at the present day. The old wretch fought lustily with death, but at length the time of his departure came. It was in the time of the barley-harvest. Two men were in a field on the cliff, a little below the house, mowing. A universal calm prevailed, and there was not a breath of wind to stir the calm. Suddenly a breeze passed by them, and they heard the words 'The time is come, but the man isn't come.' These words appeared to float in the breeze from the sea, and consequently it attracted their attention. Looking out to sea, they saw a black, heavy, square-rigged ship, with all her sails set, coming in against wind and tide, and not a hand to be seen on board. The sky became black as night around the ship, and as she came under the cliff – and she came so close to the top of the masts could scarcely be perceived – the darkness resolved itself into a lurid storm-cloud, which extended high into the air. The sun shone brilliantly over the country, except on the house of the pirate at Tregaseal – that was wrapt in the deep shadow of the cloud.

The men, in terror, left their work; they found all the neighbours gathered around the door of the pirate's cottage, none of them daring to enter it. Parson had been sent for by the terrified peasants, this divine being celebrated for his power of driving away evil spirits.

The dying wrecker was in a state of agony, crying out, in tones of the most intense terror, 'The devil is tearing at me with nails like the claws of a hawk! Put out the sailors with their bloody hands!' and using, in the paroxysms of pain, the most profane imprecations. The parson, the doctor, and two of the bravest of the fishermen were the only persons in the room. They related that at one moment the room was as dark as the grave, and that at the next it was so light that every hair on the old man's head could be seen standing on end. The parson used all his influence to dispel the evil spirit. His powers were so potent that he reduced the devil to the size of a fly, but he could not put him out of the room. All this time the room appeared as if filled with the sea, with the waves surging violently to and fro, and one could hear the breakers roaring, as if standing on the edge of the cliff in a storm. At last there was a fearful crash of thunder, and a blaze of the intensest lightning. The house appeared on fire, and the ground shook, as if with an earthquake. All rushed in terror from the house, leaving the dying man to his fate.

The storm raged with fearful violence, but appeared to contract its dimensions. The black cloud, which was first seen to come in with the black ship, was moving, with a violent internal motion, over the wrecker's house. The cloud rolled together, smaller and smaller, and suddenly, with the blast of a whirlwind, it passed from Tregaseal to the ship, and she was impelled, amidst the flashes of lightning and roarings of thunder, away over the sea.

The dead body of the pirate-wrecker lay a ghastly spectacle, with eyes expanded and the mouth partly open, still retaining the aspect of his last mortal terror. As everyone hated him, they all desired to remove his corpse as rapidly as possible from the sight of man. A rude coffin was rapidly prepared, and the body was carefully cased in its boards. They tell me the coffin was carried to the churchyard, but that it was too light to have contained the body, and that it was followed by a black pig, which joined the company forming the procession, nobody knew where, and disappeared nobody knew when. When they reached the church stile, a storm, similar in its character to that which heralded the wrecker's death, came on. The bearers of the coffin were obliged to leave it without the churchyard stile, and rush into the church for safety. The storm lasted long and raged with violence, and all was as dark as night. A sudden blaze of light, more vivid than before, was seen, and those who had the hardihood to look out saw that the lightning had set fire to the coffin, and it was being borne away through the air, blazing and whirling wildly in the grasp of such a whirlwind as no man ever witnessed before or since.

The witch of Treva

Once on a time, long ago, there lived at Treva, a hamlet in Zennor, a wonderful old lady deeply skilled in necromancy. Her charms, spells, and dark incantations made her the terror of the neighbourhood. However, this old lady failed to impress her husband with any belief in her supernatural powers nor did he fail to proclaim his unbelief aloud.

One day this sceptic came home to dinner, and found, being exceedingly hungry, to his bitter disappointment, that not only was there no dinner to eat, but that there was no meat in the house. His rage was great, but all he could get from his wife was, 'I couldn't get meat out of the stones, could I ?' It was in vain to give the reins to passion, the old woman told him, and he must know 'that hard words buttered no parsnips.'

Well, at length he resolved to put his wife's powers to the proof, and he quietly but determinedly told her that he would be the death of her if she did not get him some dinner; but if in half an hour she gave him some good cooked meat, he would believe all she had boasted of her power, and be submissive to her for ever. St Ives, the nearest market-town, was five miles off; but nothing doubting, the witch put on her bonnet and cloak, and started. Her husband watched her from their cottage door, down the hill; and at the bottom of the hill, he saw his wife quietly place herself on the ground and disappear. In her place a fine hare ran on at its full speed.

He was not a little startled, but he waited, and within the half-hour in walked his wife with 'good flesh and taties all ready for aiting'. There was no longer any doubt, and the poor husband lived in fear of the witch of Treva to the day of her death. This event took place after a few years, and it is said the room was full of evil spirits, and that the old woman's shrieks were awful to hear. Howbeit, peace in the shape of pale-faced death came to her at last, and then a black cloud rested over the house when all the heavens were clear and blue.

She was borne to the grave by six aged men, carried, as is the custom, underhand. When they were about half way between the house and the church, a hare started from the roadside and leaped over the coffin. The terrified bearers let the corpse fall to the ground, and ran away. Another lot of men took up the coffin and proceeded. They had not gone far when puss was suddenly seen seated on the coffin, and again the coffin was abandoned. After long consultation, and being persuaded by the parson to carry the old woman very quickly into the churchyard, while he walked before, six others made the attempt, and as the parson never ceased to repeat the Lord's Prayer, all went on quietly. Arrived at the church stile, they rested the corpse, the parson paused to commence the ordinary burial service, and there stood the hare, which, as soon as the clergyman began 'I am the resurrection and the life,' uttered a diabolical howl, changed into a black, unshapen creature, and disappeared.

Dorcas, the spirit of Polbreen Mine

Polbreen Mine is situated at the foot of the hill known as St Agnes Beacon. In one of the small cottages which immediately adjoins the mine once lived a woman called Dorcas. Beyond this we know little of her life; but we are concerned chiefly with her death, which, we are told, was suicidal.

From some cause, which is not related, Dorcas grew weary of life, and one unholy night she left her house and flung herself into one of the deep shafts of Polbreen Mine, at the bottom of which her dead and broken body was discovered. The remnant of humanity was brought to the surface; and after the laws of the time with regard to suicides had been fulfilled, the body of Dorcas was buried.

Her presence, however, still remained in the mine. She appears ordinarily to take a malicious delight in tormenting the industrious miner, calling him by name, and alluring him from his tasks. This was carried on by her to such an extent, that when a 'tributer' had made a poor month, he was asked if he had 'been chasing Dorcas?'

Dorcas was usually only a voice. It has been said by some that they have seen her in the mine, but this is doubted by the miners generally, who refer the spectral appearance to the fears of their comrade.

But it is stated as an incontrovertible fact, that more than one man who has met the spirit in the levels of the mine has had his clothes torn off his back; whether in anger or in sport, is not clearly made out. On one occasion, and on one occasion only, Dorcas appears to have acted kindly. Two miners, who for distinction's sake we will call Martin and Jacky, were at work in their end, and at the time busily at work 'beating the borer'.

The name of Jacky was distinctly uttered between the blows. He stopped and listened – all was still. They proceeded with their task: a blow on the iron rod. – 'Jacky.' Another blow. – 'Jacky.' They pause – all is silent. 'Well, thee wert called, Jacky,' said Martin, 'go and see.'

Jacky was, however, either afraid, or he thought himself the fool of his senses.

Work was resumed, and 'Jacky ! Jacky ! Jacky !' was called more vehemently and distinctly than before.

Jacky threw down his heavy hammer, and went from his companion, resolved to satisfy himself as to the caller.

He had not proceeded many yards from the spot on which he had been standing at work, when a mass of rock fell from the roof of the level, weighing many tons, which would have crushed him to death. Martin had been stooping, holding the borer, and a projecting corner of rock just above him turned off the falling mass. He was securely enclosed, and they had to dig him out, but he escaped without injury. Jacky declared to his dying day that he owed his life to Dorcas.

Although Dorcas's shaft remains a part of Polbreen Mine, I am informed by the agent that her presence has departed.

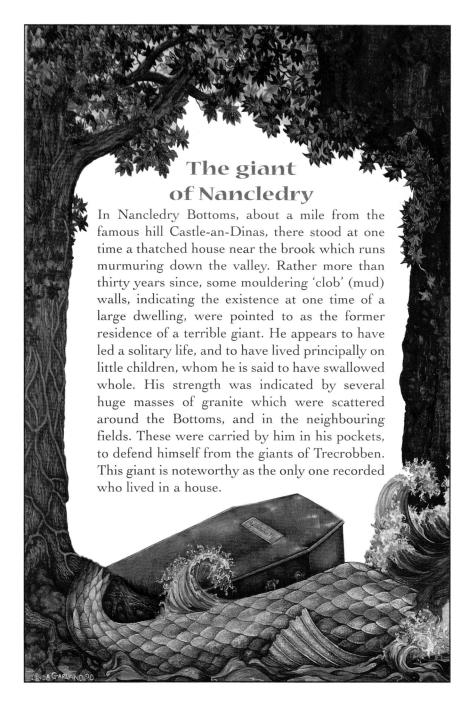

The giant of Nancledry

In Nancledry Bottoms, about a mile from the famous hill Castle-an-Dinas, there stood at one time a thatched house near the brook which runs murmuring down the valley. Rather more than thirty years since, some mouldering 'clob' (mud) walls, indicating the existence at one time of a large dwelling, were pointed to as the former residence of a terrible giant. He appears to have led a solitary life, and to have lived principally on little children, whom he is said to have swallowed whole. His strength was indicated by several huge masses of granite which were scattered around the Bottoms, and in the neighbouring fields. These were carried by him in his pockets, to defend himself from the giants of Trecrobben. This giant is noteworthy as the only one recorded who lived in a house.

The Dead Hand

I've seen it – I've seen it!' exclaimed a young woman, pale with terror, approaching with much haste the door of a cottage, around which were gathered several of the miners' wives inhabiting the adjoining dwellings.

'God's mercy be with the cheild!' replied the oldest woman of the group, with very great seriousness.

'Aunt Alice,' asked one of the youngest women, 'and do 'e b'lieve any harm will come o' seeing it?'

'Mary Doble saw it and pined; Jinny Trestrail was never the same woman after she seed the hand in Wheal Jewel; and I knows ever so many more; but let us hope, by the blessing o' the Lord, no evil will come on Mary.'

Mary was evidently impressed with a sense of some heavy trouble. She sighed deeply and pressed her hand to her side, as if to still the beating of her heart. The thoughtless faith of the old woman promised to work out a fulfilment of her fears in producing mental distress and corporeal suffering in the younger one.

While this was passing in the little village, a group of men were gathered around a deserted shaft, which existed in too dangerous proximity with the abodes of the miners. They were earnestly discussing the question of the reality of the appearance of the *dead hand* – those who had not seen it expressing a doubt of its reality, while others declared most emphatically that 'in that very shaft they had seed 'un with a lighted candle in his hand, moving up and down upon the ladders, as though he was carried by a living man.'

It appears that some time previously to the abandonment of the mine, an unfortunate miner was ascending from his subterranean labours, carrying his candle in his hand. He was probably seized with giddiness, but from that or some other cause he fell away from the ladders, and was found by his comrades a bleeding corpse at the bottom.

The character of this man was not of the best; and after his burial, it was stated by the people that he had been seen. From a vague rumour of his spectral appearance on the surface, the tale eventually settled itself into that of the dead hand, moving up and down in the shaft.

By the spectral light of the candle, the hand had been distinctly visible to many, and the irregular motion of the light proved that the candle was held in the usual manner between the thumb and finger in its ball of clay, while the fingers were employed in grasping stave after stave of the ladder. The belief in the evil attendant on being unfortunate enough to see this spectral hand prevailed very generally amongst the mining population about twenty years since [c1840]. The dead hand was not, however, confined to one shaft or mine. Similar narrations have been met with in several districts.

The Ghost of Rosewarne

Ezekiel Grosse, Gent., attorney-at-law, bought the lands of Rosewarne from one of the De Rosewarnes, who had become involved in difficulties by endeavouring without sufficient means to support the dignity of his family. There is reason for believing that Ezekiel was the legal advisor of this unfortunate Rosewarne, and that he was not over-honest in his transactions with his client. However this may be, Ezekiel Grosse had scarcely made Rosewarne his dwelling-place before he was alarmed by noises, at first of an unearthly character, and subsequently one very dark night by the appearance of the ghost himself in the form of a worn and aged man. The first appearance was in the park, but he subsequently repeated his visits in the house, but always after dark. Ezekiel Grosse was not a man to be terrified by trifles, and for some time he paid but slight attention to his nocturnal visitor. Howbeit, the repetition of visits, and certain mysterious indications on the part of the spectre, became annoying to Ezekiel.

One night, when seated in his office examining some deeds, and being rather irritable, having lost an important suit, his visitor approached him, making some strange indications which the lawyer could not understand. Ezekiel suddenly exclaimed, 'In the name of God, what wantest thou?'

'To show thee, Ezekiel Grosse, where the gold for which thou longest lies buried.'

No one ever lived upon whom the greed of gold was stronger than on Ezekiel, yet he hesitated now that his spectral friend had spoken so plainly, and trembled in every limb as the ghost slowly delivered himself in sepulchral tones of this telling speech.

The lawyer looked fixedly on the spectre, but he dared not utter a word. He longed to obtain possession of the secret, yet he feared to ask him where he was to find this treasure. The spectre looked as fixedly at the poor trembling lawyer, as if enjoying the sight of his terror. At length, lifting his finger, he beckoned Ezekiel to follow him, turning at the same time to leave the room. Ezekiel was glued to his seat; he could not exert strength enough to move although he desired to do so.

'Come!' said the ghost in a hollow voice. The lawyer was powerless to come.

'Gold!' exclaimed the old man in a whining tone, though in a louder key.

'Where?' gasped Ezekiel.

'Follow me, and I will show thee,' said the ghost. Ezekiel endeavoured to rise but it was in vain.

'I command thee, come!' almost shrieked the ghost. Ezekiel felt that he was compelled to follow his friend, and by some supernatural power rather than his own, he followed the spectre out of the room and through the hall into the park.

They passed onward through the night – the ghost gliding before the lawyer, and guiding him by a peculiar phosphorescent light, which appeared to glow from every part of the form, until they arrived at a little dell, and had reached a small cairn formed of granite boulders. By this the spectre rested; when Ezekiel had approached it, and was standing on the other side of the cairn, still trembling, the aged man, looking fixedly in his face, said in low tones, 'Ezekiel Grosse, thou longest for gold as I did. I won the glittering prize but I could not enjoy it. Heaps of treasure are buried beneath those stones; it is thine, if thou diggest for it. Win the gold, Ezekiel. Glitter with the wicked ones of the world; and when thou art the most joyous, I will look in upon thy happiness.'

The ghost then disappeared, and as soon as Grosse could recover himself from the extreme trepidation – the result of mixed feelings – he looked about him, and finding himself alone, he exclaimed 'Ghost or devil, I will soon prove whether or not thou liest!' Ezekiel is said to have heard a laugh, echoing between the hills, as he said those words.

The lawyer noted well the spot; returned to his house, pondered on all the circumstances of his case, and eventually resolved to seize the earliest opportunity, when he might do so unobserved, of removing the stones and examining the ground beneath them.

A few nights after this, Ezekiel went to the little cairn, and by the aid of a crowbar he soon overturned the stones and laid the ground bare. He then commenced digging, and had not proceeded far when his spade struck against some other metal. He carefully cleared away the earth, and then he felt – for he could not see, having no light with him, that he had uncovered a metallic urn of some kind. He found it quite impossible to lift it, and he was therefore compelled to cover it up again, and to replace the stones sufficiently to hide it from the observation of any chance wanderer.

The next night Ezekiel found that this urn, which was of bronze, contained gold coins of a very ancient date. He loaded himself with his treasure and returned home. From time to time, at night, as Ezekiel found he could do so without exciting the suspicions of his servants, he visited the urn and thus by degrees removed all the treasure to Rosewarne House. There was nothing in the series of circumstances which had surrounded Ezekiel which he could less understand than the fact that the ghost of the old man had left off troubling him from the moment when he had disclosed to him the hiding place of this treasure.

The neighbouring gentry could not but observe the rapid improvements which Ezekiel Grosse made in his mansion, in his grounds, in his personal appearance, and indeed in everything by which he was surrounded. In a short time he abandoned the law and led in every respect the life of a country gentleman. He ostentatiously paraded his power to procure all earthly enjoyments and, in spite of his notoriously bad character, he succeeded in drawing many of the landed proprietors around him.

Things went well with Ezekiel. The man who could in those days visit London in his own carriage and four was not without a large circle of flatterers. The lawyer who had struggled hard in the outset of life to secure wealth, and who did not always employ the most honest means for doing so, now found himself in the centre of a circle to whom he could preach honesty, and receive from them expressions of the admiration in which the world holds the possessor of gold. His old tricks were forgotten and he was put in places of honour. This state of things continued for some time; indeed, Grosse's entertainments became more and more splendid, and his revels more and more seductive to those who were admitted to share them with him. The lord of Rosewarne was the lord of the west. To him everyone bowed the knee: he walked the earth as the proud possessor of a large share of the planet.

It was Christmas Eve and a large gathering there was at Rosewarne. In the hall the ladies and gentlemen were in the full enjoyment of the dance, and in the kitchen all the tenantry and the servants were emulating their superiors. Everything went joyously; when mirth was in full swing, and Ezekiel felt to the full the influence of wealth, it appeared as if in one moment the chill of death had fallen over everyone. The dancers paused and looked one at another, each one struck with the other's paleness; there, in the middle of the hall, everyone saw a strange old man looking angrily, but in silence, at Ezekiel Grosse, who was fixed in terror, blank as a statue.

No one had seen this old man enter the hall, yet there he was in the midst of them. It was but for a minute and he was gone. Ezekiel, as if a frozen torrent of water had thawed in an instant, roared with impetuous laughter.

'What do you think of that for a Christmas play? There was an old Father Christmas for you! Ha-ha! Ha-ha! How frightened you all look! Butler, order the men to hand round the spiced wines! On with the dancing my friends! It was only a trick, ay, and a clever one which I put upon you. On with your dancing my friends!'

Notwithstanding his boisterous attempts to restore the spirit of the evening, Ezekiel could not succeed. There was an influence stronger than any which he could command; and one by one, framing sundry excuses, his guests took their departure, every one of them satisfied that all was not right at Rosewarne.

From that Christmas Eve Grosse was a changed man. He tried to be his former self; but it was in vain. Again and again he called his gay companions around him; but at every feast there appeared one more than was desired. An aged man – weird beyond measure – took his place at the table in the middle of the feast; and although he spoke not, he exerted a miraculous power over all. No one dared to move; no one ventured to speak. Occasionally Ezekiel assumed an appearance of courage, which he felt not; rallied his guests and made sundry excuses for the presence of his aged friend, whom he represented as having a mental infirmity, as being deaf and dumb. On all such occasions the old man rose from the table and, looking at the host, laughed a demoniac laugh of joy, and departed as quietly as he came.

The natural consequence of this was that Ezekiel Grosse's friends fell away from him, and he became a lonely man, amidst his vast possessions – his only companion being his faithful clerk, John Call.

The persecuting presence of the spectre became more and more constant; and wherever the poor lawyer went, there was the aged man at his side. From being one of the finest men in the county he became a miserably attenuated and bowed old man. Misery was stamped on every feature – terror was indicated in every movement. At length he appears to have besought his ghostly attendant to free him of his presence. It was long before the ghost would listen to any terms; but when Ezekiel at length agreed to surrender the whole of his wealth to anyone whom the spectre might indicate, he obtained a promise that upon this being carried out, in a perfectly legal manner, in favour of John Call, he should no longer be haunted.

This was, after numerous struggles on the part of Ezekiel to retain his property, or at least some portion of it, legally settled, and John Call became possessor of Rosewarne and the adjoining lands. Grosse was then informed that this evil spirit was one of the ancestors of the De

Rosewarne from whom by his fraudulent dealings he obtained the place, and that he was allowed to visit the earth again for the purpose of inflicting the most condign punishment on the avaricious lawyer.

His avarice had been gratified, his pride had been pampered to the highest; and then he was made a pitiful spectacle, at whom all men pointed and no one pitied.

He lived on in misery, but it was for a short time. He was found dead, and the country people ever said that his death was a violent one; they spoke of marks on his body, and some even asserted that the spectre of De Rosewarne was seen rejoicing amidst a crowd of devils, as they bore the spirit of Ezekiel over Carn Brea.

The voice from the sea

A fisherman or a pilot was walking one night on the sands at Porth-Town, when all was still save the monotonous fall of the light waves upon the sand. He distinctly heard a voice from the sea exclaiming, — 'The hour is come, but not the man.' This was repeated three times, when a black figure, like that of a man, appeared on the top of the hill. It paused for a moment, then rushed impetuously down the steep incline, over the sands, and was lost in the sea. In different forms this story is told all around the Cornish coast.

The White Hare

It is a very popular fancy that when a maiden, who has loved not wisely but too well, dies forsaken and broken-hearted, she comes back to haunt her deceiver in the form of a white hare. This phantom follows the false one everywhere, mostly invisible to all but him. It sometimes saves him from danger, but invariably the white hare causes the death of the betrayer in the end.

A large landed proprietor once engaged a fine, handsome young fellow to manage his farm, which was very extensive as well as a high-class one. When the young farmer was duly settled in his new farmhouse, there came to live with him, to take the management of the dairy, a peasant's daughter. She was very handsome, and of a singularly fine figure, but entirely without education.

The farmer became desperately in love with this young creature, and eventually their love passed all the bounds of discretion. It became the policy of the young farmer's family to put down this unfortunate passion by substituting a more legitimate and endearing object.

After a long trial, they thought they were successful and the young farmer was married.

Many months had not passed away when the discharged dairy-maid was observed to suffer from illness, which, however, she constantly spoke of as nothing; but knowing dames saw too clearly the truth. One morning there was found in a field a newly-born babe, strangled. The unfortunate girl was at once suspected as being the parent, and the evidence was soon sufficient to charge her with the murder. She was tried, and chiefly by the evidence of the young farmer and his family, convicted of, and executed for, the murder.

Everything now went wrong in the farm, and the young man suddenly left it and went into another part of the country.

Still nothing prospered, and he gradually took to drink to drown some secret sorrow. He was more frequently on the road by night than by day; and, go where he would, a white hare was constantly crossing his path. The white hare was often seen by others, almost always under the feet of his horse; and the poor terrified animal would go like the wind to avoid the strange apparition.

One morning the young farmer was found drowned in a forsaken mine; and the horse, which had evidently suffered extreme terror, was grazing near the corpse. Beyond all doubt the white hare, which is known to hunt the perjured and the false-hearted to death, had terrified the horse to such a degree that eventually the rider was thrown into the mine-waste in which the body was found.

Phantoms of the Dying

A gay party were assembled one afternoon, in the latter days of January, in the best parlour of a farmhouse near the Land's End. The inhabitants of this district were, in many respects, peculiar. Nearly all the land was divided up between comparatively few owners, and every owner lived on and farmed his own land.

This circumstance, amongst others, led to a certain amount of style in many of the old farmhouses of the Land's End district; and even now, in some of them from which, alas!, the glory has departed, may be seen the evidences of taste beyond that which might have been expected in so remote a district.

The 'best parlour' was frequently panelled with carved oak, and the ceiling often highly, though it must be admitted heavily, decorated. In such a room, in the declining light of a January afternoon, were some ten or a dozen farmers' daughters, all of them unmarried, and many of them having an eye on the farmer's eldest son, a fine young man about twenty years of age, called Joseph.

The farmer and his wife, at the time of which we speak, had three sons and two daughters. The eldest son was an excellent and amiable young man, possessed of many personal attractions, and especially fond of the society of his sisters and their friends. The next son was of a very different stamp, and was more frequently found at the inn at Church-town than at his father's house; the youngest son was an apprentice at Penzance. The two daughters, Mary and Honour, had coaxed their mother into a 'tea and heavy-cake party' and Joseph was especially retained to be, as everyone said he was, 'the life of the company'.

In those days when, especially in those parts, everyone took dinner at noon and tea not much after four o'clock, the party had assembled early.

There had been the usual preliminary gossip among the young people, when they began to talk about the wreck of a fruit-ship, which had occurred but a few days before, off the Land's End, and it was said that considerable quantities of oranges were washing into Nanjizal Cove. Upon this, Joseph said he would take one of the men from the farm, and go down to the Cove – which was not far off – and see if they could find some oranges for the ladies.

The day had faded into twilight, the western sky was still bright with the light of the setting sun, and the illuminated clouds shed a certain portion of their splendour into the room in which the party were assembled. The girls were divided up into groups, having their own pretty little bits of gossip, often truly delightful from its entire freedom and its innocence; and the mother of Joseph was seated near the fireplace, looking with some anxiety through the windows, from which she commanded a view of the Atlantic Ocean. The old lady was restless; sometimes she had to whisper something to Mary and then some other thing to Honour.

Her anxiety, at length, was expressed in her wondering where Joseph could be tarrying so long. All the young ladies sought to ease her mind by saying that there were no doubt so many orange-gatherers in the Cove that Joseph and the man could not get so much fruit as he desired.

Joseph was the favourite son of his mother, and her anxiety evidently increased. Eventually, starting from her chair, the old lady exclaimed, 'Oh, here he is; now I'll see about the tea.'

With a pleased smile on her face she left the room, to return, however, to it in deeper sorrow.

The mother expected to meet her son at the door – he came not. Thinking that he might possibly have been wetted by the sea, and that he had gone round the house to another door leading directly into the kitchen, for the purpose of drying himself, or of changing his boots, she went into the dairy to fetch the basin of clotted cream, which had been 'taken up' with unusual care to see if the junket was properly set, and to spread the flaky cream thickly upon its surface.

Strange – as the old lady subsequently related – all the pans of milk were agitated – 'the milk rising up and down like the waves of the sea'.

The anxious mother returned to the parlour with the basin of cream, but with an indescribable feeling of an unknown terror. She commanded herself, and, in her usual quiet way, asked if Joseph had been in. When they answered her 'No,' she sighed heavily and sank senseless into a chair.

Neither Joseph nor the servant returned alive. They were seen standing together upon a rock, stooping to gather oranges as they came with each wave up to their feet, when one of the heavy swells – the lingering undulations of a tempest, so well known on this coast – came sweeping onward, and carried them both away in its cave of waters, as the wave curved to engulf them.

The undertow of the tidal current was so strong that, though powerful men and good swimmers, they were carried at once beyond all human aid and speedily perished.

The house of joy became a house of mourning, and sadness rested on it for years. Day after day passed by and, although a constant watch was kept along the coast, it was not until the fated ninth day that the bodies were discovered, and they were then found in sadly mutilated state.

Often after long years, and when the consolations derivable from pure religious feeling had brought that tranquillity upon the mind of this loving mother, which so much resembles the poetical repose of an autumnal evening, has she repeated to me the sad tale.

Again and again I have heard her declare that she saw Joseph, her son, as distinctly as ever she saw him in her life, and that, as he passed the parlour windows, he looked in upon her and smiled.

The Smuggler's Token

Until about the time of the close of the last French war, a large portion of the inhabitants of the south-west coast of Cornwall were in some way or another connected with the practice of smuggling. The traffic with the opposite coast was carried on principally in boats or undecked vessels. The risks encountered by their crews produced a race of hardy, fearless men, a few of whom are still living, and it has been said that the government of those days winked at the infraction of the law, from an unwillingness to destroy so excellent a school of seamen. Recently the demand for ardent spirits has so fallen off, that there is no longer an inducement to smuggle; still it is sometimes exultingly rumoured that 'the Coast Guard having been cleverly put off the scent, a cargo has been successfully run'. The little coves in the Lizard promontory formed the principal trading places, the goods being taken as soon as landed to various places of concealment, whence they were withdrawn as required for disposal.

About 80 years since, a boat, laden with ankers of spirits, was about, with its crew, to leave Mullion for Newlyn. One of the farmers concerned in the venture, members of whose family are still living, was persuaded to accompany them, and entered the boat for that purpose, but, recollecting he had business at Helston, got out again and the boat left without him. On his return from Helston, late in the evening, he sat down exclaiming, 'The boat and all on board her are lost! I met the men as I passed the top of Halzephron [a very high cliff on the road] with their hair and clothes dripping wet!' In spite of the arguments of his friends, he persisted in his statement. The boat and crew were never more heard of, and the farmer was so affected by the circumstance that he pined and died shortly after.

The Pilot's Ghost Story

I prefer giving this story in the words in which it was communicated. For its singular character, it's a ghost story well worth preserving.

'Just seventeen years since, I went down on the wharf from my house one night between about twelve and one in the morning, to see whether there was any "hobble" and found a sloop, the *Sally* of St Ives [the *Sally* was wrecked at St Ives one Saturday afternoon in the Spring of 1862], in the bay, bound for Hayle. When I got by the White Hart public house I saw a man leaning against a post on the wharf. I spoke to him, wished him good morning, and asked him what o'clock it was, but to no purpose. I was not to be easily frightened, for I did not believe in ghosts; and finding I got no answer to my repeated enquiries, I approached close to him and said, "Thee'rt a queer sort of fellow, not to speak; I'd speak to the devil if he were to speak to me. Who art a at all? Thee'st needn't think to frighten me; that thee wasn't do, if thou wert twice so ugly; who art a at all?' He turned his great ugly face on me, glared abroad his great eyes, opened his mouth, and it was a mouth sure nuff. Then I saw pieces of seaweed and bits of stick in his whiskers; the flesh of his face and hands were par-boiled, just like a woman's hands after a good day's washing. Well, I did not like his looks a bit, and sheered off; but he followed close by my side, and I could hear the water squashing in his shoes every step he took. Well, I stopped a bit and thought to be a little bit civil to him, and spoke to him again, but no answer. I then thought I would go to seek for another of our crew, and knock him up to get the vessel, and had got about fifty or sixty yards when I turned to see if he was following me, but saw him where I left him. Fearing he would come after me, I ran for my life the few steps that I had to go. But when I got to the door, to my horror there stood the man in the door, grinning horribly. I shook like an aspen leaf; my hat lifted from my head; the sweat boiled out of me. What to do I don't know, and in the house there was such a row, as if everybody was breaking up everything. After a bit I went in, for the door was on the latch and called the captain of the boat, and got lights, but everything was all right, nor had he heard any noise. We went out aboard of the *Sally* and I put her into Hayle, but I felt ill enough to be in bed. I left the vessel to come home as soon as I could, but it took me four hours to walk two miles, and I had to lie down in the road, and was taken home to St Ives in a cart as far as the Terrace; from there I was carried by my brothers and put to bed. Three days afterwards all my hair fell off as if I'd had my head shaved. The roots, and for about half an inch from the roots, being quite white. I was ill six months, and the doctor's bill was £4 17s. 6d. for attendance and medicine. So you see I have reason to believe in the existence of spirits as much as Mr Wesley had. My hair grew again, and twelve months after I had as good a head of dark brown hair as ever.'

The Execution and Wedding

A woman, who had lived at Ludgvan, was executed at Bodmin for the murder of her husband. There was but little doubt that she had been urged on to the diabolical deed by a horse-dealer, known as Yorkshire Jack, with whom, for a long period, she was generally supposed to have been criminally acquainted.

One morning, during my residence in Penzance, an old woman from Ludgvan called on me with some trifling message. While she was waiting for my answer, I made some ordinary remark about the weather.

'It's all owing to Sarah Polgrain,' said she.
'Sarah Polgrain!' said I; 'and who is Sarah Polgrain?'

Then the voluble old lady told me the whole story of the poisoning, with which we need not at present concern ourselves. By and by the tale grew especially interesting, and there I resume it.

Sarah had begged that Yorkshire Jack might accompany her to the scaffold when she was led forward to execution. This was granted; and on the dreadful morning there stood this unholy pair, the fatal beam on which the woman's body was in a few minutes to swing, before them.

They kissed each other, and whispered words passed between them.

The executioner intimated that the moment of execution had arrived, and they must part. Sarah Polgrain, looking earnestly into the man's eyes, said 'You will?'

Yorkshire Jack replied, 'I will!' Then they separated. The man retired amongst the crowd, the woman was soon a dead corpse, pendulating in the wind.

Years passed on. Yorkshire Jack was never the same man as before, his whole bearing was altered. His bold, his dashing air deserted him. He walked, or rather wandered, slowly about the streets of the town, or the lanes of the country. He constantly moved his head from side to side, looking first over one, then over the other shoulder, as though dreading that someone was following him. The stout man became thin, his ruddy cheeks more pale, and his eyes sunken.

At length he disappeared, and it was discovered – for Yorkshire Jack had made a confidant of some Ludgvan man – that he had pledged himself 'living or dead to become the husband of Sarah Polgrain, after the lapse of years'.

To escape, if possible, from himself, Jack had gone to sea in the merchant service.

Well, the period had arrived when this unholy promise was to be fulfilled. Yorkshire Jack was returning from the Mediterranean in a fruit-ship. He was met by the devil and Sarah Polgrain far out at sea, off the Land's End. Jack would not accompany them willingly; so they followed the ship for days, during all which time she was involved in a storm. Eventually Jack was washed from the deck by such a wave as the oldest sailor had never seen; and presently, amidst loud thunders and flashing lightnings, riding as it were in a dark cloud, three figures were seen passing onward. These were the devil, Sarah Polgrain, and Yorkshire Jack; and this was the cause of the storm.

'It is all true, as you may learn if you will inquire,' said the old woman, 'for many of her kin live in Church-town.'

Duffy and the Devil

It was in cider-making time. Squire Lovel of Trove, or more correctly Trewoof, rode up to Buryan church-town to procure help. Boys and maidens were in request, some to gather the apples from the trees, others to carry them to the cider mill. Passing along the village as hastily as the dignity of a squire would allow him, his attention was drawn to a great noise – scolding in a shrill treble voice, and crying – proceeding from Janey Chygwin's door.

The squire rode up to the cottage, and he saw the old woman beating her step-daughter Duffy about the head with the skirt of her swing-tail gown, in which she had been carrying out the ashes. She had made such a dust that the squire was nearly choked and almost blinded with the wood ashes.

'What cheer, Janey?' cried the squire; 'what's the to-do with you and Duffy?'

'Oh!' shouts Janey, 'the lazy hussy is all her time courseying and couranting with the boys! She will never stay in to boil the porridge, knit the stockings, or spin the yarn.'

'Don't believe her, your honour,' exclaims Duffy; 'my knitting and spinning is the best in the parish.'

The war of tongues continued in this strain for some time, the old squire looking calmly on and resolving in his mind to take Duffy home with him to Trove, her appearance evidently pleasing him greatly. Squire Lovel left the old and young woman to do the best they could, and went around the village to complete his hiring. When he returned, peace had been declared between them; but when Lovel expressed his desire to take Duffy home to his house to help the housekeeper do the spinning, 'A pretty spinner she is!' shouted old Janey at the top of her voice.

'Try me, your honour,' said Duffy, curtseying very low; 'my yarns are the best in the parish.'

'We'll soon try that,' said the squire. 'Janey will be glad to get quits of thee, I see, and thou'lt be nothing loath to leave her, so jump up behind me, Duffy.'

No sooner said than done. The maid Duffy, without ceremony, mounted behind the squire on the horse, and they jogged silently down to Trove.

Squire Lovel's old housekeeper was almost blind – one eye had been put out by an angry old wizard – and through sympathy she was rapidly losing the other.

This old dame was consequently very glad of someone to help her with spinning and knitting.

The introduction over, the housekeeper takes Duffy up into the garret where the wool was kept, and where the spinning was done in the summer, and requests her to commence her work.

The truth must be told: Duffy was an idle slut, she could neither knit nor spin. Well, here she was left alone, and, of course, expected to produce a good specimen of her work.

The garret was piled from the floor to key-beams with fleeces of wool. Duffy looked despairingly at them, then sat herself down on the 'turn' – the spinning wheel – and cried out 'Curse the spinning and knitting! The devil may spin and knit for the squire for all I care.'

Scarcely had Duffy spoken these words when she heard a queer rustling noise behind some wool-packs, and forth walked a queer-looking little man with a remarkable pair of eyes, which seemed to send out flashes of light. There was something uncommonly knowing in the twist of his mouth and his curved nose had an air of curious intelligence. He was dressed in black, and moved towards Duffy with a jaunty air, knocking something against the floor with every step he took.

'Duffy dear,' said this little gentleman, I'll do all the spinning and knitting for thee.'

'Thank'ee,' says Duffy, quite astonished.

'Duffy dear, a lady shall you be.'

'Thank'ee, your honour,' smiled Duffy.

'But, Duffy dear, remember,' coaxingly said the queer little man, 'remember, that for all this, at the end of three years, you must go with me, unless you can find out my name.'

Duffy was not the least bit frightened, nor did she hesitate long, but presently struck a bargain with her kind but unknown friend, who told her she had only to wish, and her every wish should be fulfilled; and as for the spinning and knitting, she would find all she required under the black ram's fleece.

He then departed. How, Duffy could not tell, but in a moment the queer little gentleman had gone.

Duffy sung in idleness and slept until it was time for her to make her appearance. So she wished for some yarns, and looking under the black fleece she found them.

Those were shown by the housekeeper to the squire, and both declared they had never seen such beautiful yarns.

The next day Duffy was to knit this yarn into stockings. Duffy idled as only professed idlers can idle; but in due time, as if she had been excessively industrious, she produced a pair of stockings for the old squire.

If the yarn was beautiful, the stockings were beyond all praise. they were as fine as silk and as strong as leather. Squire Lovel soon gave them a trial; and when he came home again at night after hunting, he declared he would never wear any other than Duffy's stockings. He had wandered all day through brake and briar, furze and brambles; there was not a scratch on his legs, and he was as dry as a bone. There was no end to his praise of Duffy's stockings.

Duffy had a rare time of it now – she could do what she pleased and rove where she willed.

She was dancing on the mill-bed half the day, with all the gossiping women who brought their grist to be ground. In those 'good old times' the ladies of the parish would take their corn to mill, and serge the flour themselves. When a few of them met together, they would either tell stories or dance whilst the corn was grinding. Sometimes the dance would be on the mill-bed, sometimes out on the green. On some occasions the miller's fiddle would be in request, at others the 'crowd' [a sieve covered with sheepskin] was made to do the duty of a tambourine.

So Duffy was always finding excuses to go to mill and many a round would she dance with the best in the parish.

Old Bet, the miller's wife, was a witch, and she found out who did Duffy's work for her. Duffy and old Bet were always the best of friends, and she never told anyone of Duffy's knitting friend, nor did she ever say a word about the stockings being unfinished. *There was always a stitch down.*

On Sundays the people went to Buryan church from all parts, to look at the squire's stockings, and the old squire would stop at the cross, proud enough to show them. He could hunt
Through brambles and furze in all sorts of weather;
His old shanks were as sound as if bound up in leather.

Duffy was now sought after by all the young men of the country; and at last the squire, fearing to lose a pretty girl and one who was so useful to him, married her himself, and she became, according to the fashion of the time and place, Lady Lovel; but she was commonly known by her neighbours as Duffy Lady.

Lady Lovel kept the devil hard at work. Stockings, all sorts of fine underclothing, bedding, and much ornamental work, the like of which was never seen, was produced at command and passed off as her own.

Duffy passed a merry time of it, but somehow or other she was never happy when she was compelled to play the lady. She passed much more of her time with the old crone at the mill than in the drawing room at Trove. The squire sported and drank, and cared little about Duffy, as long as she provided him with knitted garments.

The three years were nearly at an end. Duffy had tried every plan to find out the devil's name, but had failed at all.

She began to fear that she would have to go off with her queer friend, and Duffy became melancholy. Old Bet endeavoured to rouse her, persuading her that she could from her long experience and many dealings with the imps of darkness, at the last moment put her in the way of escaping her doom.

Duffy went day after day to her garret, and there each day was the devil gibing and jeering till she was almost mad.

There was but another day. Bet was seriously consulted now, and, as good as her word, she promised to use her power. Duffy Lady was to bring down to the mill that evening a jack of the strongest beer she had in the cellar. She was not to go to bed until the squire returned from hunting, no matter how late, and she was to make no remark in reply to anything the squire might tell her.

The jack of beer was duly carried to the mill, and Duffy returned home very melancholy to wait up for the squire.

No sooner had Lady Lovel left the mill than old Bet came out with the crowd over her shoulders and the blackjack in her hand. She shut the door and turned the water off the mill-wheel – threw her red cloak about her, and away.

She was seen by her neighbours going towards Boleit. A man saw the old woman trudging past the Pipers, and through the Dawnse Main into the downs, but there he lost sight of her, and no one could tell where old Bet had gone to at that time of night.

Duffy waited long and anxiously. By and by the dogs came home alone. They were covered with foam, their tongues were hanging out of their mouths, and all the servants said they must have met the devil's hounds without heads.

Duffy was seriously alarmed. Midnight came but no squire. At last he arrived, but like a crazy, crack-brained man he kept singing:
Here's to the devil,
With his wooden pick and shovel.

He was neither drunk nor frightened, but wild with some strange excitement. After a long time Squire Lovel sat down, and began, 'My dear Duffy, you haven't smiled this long time; but now I'll tell 'e something that would make ye laugh if ye were dying. If you'd seen what I've seen tonight, ha, ha, ha!'
Here's to the devil,
With his wooden pick and shovel.

True to her orders Duffy said not a word, but allowed the squire to ramble on as he pleased. At length he told her the following story of his adventures, with interruptions which have not been retained and with numerous coarse expressions which are best forgotten:

'Duffy dear, I left home at the break of day this morning. I hunted all the moors from Trove to Trevider, and never started a hare all the livelong day. I determined to hunt all night, but that I'd have a brace to bring home. So, at nightfall I went to Lamorna Bottoms, then up Brene Downses, and as we passed the Dawnse Main up started a hare, as fine a hare as ever was seen. She passed the Pipers, down through the Reens, in the mouth of the dogs half the time, yet they couldn't catch her at all. As fine a chase as ever was seen, until she took into the Fugoe Hole*****. In went the dogs after her, and I followed, the owls and bats flying round my head. On we went, through water and mud, a mile or more, I'm quite certain. I didn't know the place was so long before. At last we came to a broad pool of water, when the dogs lost the scent and ran back past me, howling and jowling, terrified almost to death! A little further on I turned round a corner, and saw a glimmering fire on the other side of the water, and there were St Levan witches in scores. Some were riding on ragwort, some on brooms, some were floating on their three-legged stools, and some, who had been milking the little good cows in Wales, had come back astride of the largest leeks they could find. Amongst the rest, there was our Bet of the Mill, with her crowd in her hand and my own blackjack slung across her shoulders.

'In a short time the witches gathered round the fire, and blew it up, after a strange fashion, till it burned up into a brilliant blue flame. Then I saw amongst the rest a queer little man in black, with a long forked tail which he held high in the air, and twirled around. Bet struck her crowd as soon as he appeared, and beat up the tune:

Here's to the devil,
With his wooden pick and shovel.
Digging tin by the bushel,
With his tail cock'd up.

'Then the queer little devil and all danced like the wind, and went faster and faster, making such a clatter as if they had on each foot a pewter platter.

'Every time the man in black came round by old Bet, he took a good pull from my own blackjack, till at last, as if he had been drinking my best beer, he seemed to have lost his head, when he jumped up and down, turned round and round, and roaring with laughter sung:

Duffy, my lady, you'll never know – what? –
That my name is Terrytop, Terrytop – top!'

When the squire sung those lines, he stopped suddenly, thinking that Duffy was going to die. She turned pale and red, and pale again. However Duffy said nothing, and the squire proceeded:

'After the dance, all the witches made a ring around the fire, and again blew it up, until the blue flames reached the top of the zawn [a cavernous gorge]. Then the devil danced through and through the fire, and springing ever and anon amongst the witches, kicked them soundly. At last – I was shaking with laughter at the fun – I shouted, "Go it, Old Nick!" and, lo, the lights went out and I had to fly with all my speed, for every one of the witches were after me. I scampered home somehow, and here I am. Why don't you laugh, Duffy?' Duffy did laugh, and laugh right heartily now, and when tired of their fun the squire and his lady went to bed.

The three years were up within an hour. Duffy had willed for an abundant supply of knitted things, and filled every chest in the house. She was in the best chamber, trying to cram some more stockings into a big chest, when the queer little man in black appeared as expected before her.

'Well, Duffy my dear,' said he, 'I have been to my word, and served you truly for three years as we agreed, so now I hope you will go with me and make no objection.' He bowed very obsequiously, almost down to the ground, and regarded Duffy Lady with a very offensive leer.

'I fear,' smiled Duffy, 'that your country is rather warm, and might spoil my fair complexion.'

'It is not so hot as some people say, Duffy,' was his reply. 'but come along, I've kept my word, and of course a lady of your standing will keep your word also. Can you tell me my name?'

Duffy curtsied, and smilingly said, 'You have behaved like a true gentleman; yet I wouldn't like to go so far.' The devil frowned, and approached as if he would lay forcible hands upon her. 'Maybe your name is Lucifer?'

He stamped his foot and grinned horridly. 'Lucifer! Lucifer! He's no other than a servant to me in my own country.' Suddenly calming again, he said quietly, 'Lucifer! I would scarcely be seen speaking to him at court. But come along. When I spin for ladies I expect honourable treatment at their hands. You have two guesses more. But they're of little use; my name is not generally known on earth.'

'Perhaps,' smiled Duffy again, 'my lord's name is Beelzebub?'

How he grinned, and his sides shook with convulsive joy. 'Beelzebub,' says he; 'why, he's little better than the other, a common devil he. I believe he's some sort of a cousin – a Cornish cousin you know.'

'I hope your honour,' curtsied Duffy, 'will not take offence. Impute my mistake to ignorance.'

Our demon was rampant with joy; he danced around Duffy with delight, and was, seeing that she hesitated, about to seize her somewhat roughly.

'Stop! Stop!' shouts Duffy. 'Perhaps you will be honest enough to admit that your name is Terrytop.'

The gentleman in black looked at Duffy, and she steadily looked him in the face. 'Terrytop! Deny it if you dare,' says she.

'A gentleman never denies his name,' replied Terrytop, drawing himself up with much dignity. I did not expect to be beaten by a young minx like you, Duffy; but the pleasure of your company is merely postponed.' With this Terrytop departed in fire and smoke, and all the devil's knitting suddenly turned to ashes.

Squire Lovel was out hunting, away far on the moors; the day was cold and the winds piercing. Suddenly the stockings dropped from his legs and the homespun from his back, so that he came home with nothing on but his shirt and his shoes, almost dead with cold. All this was attributed by the squire to the influence of old Bet, who, he thought, had punished him for pursuing her with his dogs when she had assumed the form of a hare.

---

* Footnote:

There is a tradition, firmly believed on the lower side of Buryan, that the Fugoe Hole extends from the cliffs underground so far that the end of it is under the parlour of the Tremewens' house in Trove, which is the only remaining portion of the old mansion of the Lovels.

Here the witches were in the habit of meeting the devil, and holding their Sabbath. Often his dark Highness has been heard piping, while the witches danced to his music. A pool of water some distance from the entrance prevents an adventurer from exploring the 'Hole' to its termination. Hares often take refuge in the Fugoe Hole, from which they have never been known to return.

Sir Francis Drake and his Demon

Sir Francis Drake – who appears to have been especially befriended by his demon – is said to drive at night a black hearse drawn by headless horses, and urged on by running devils and yelping, headless dogs, through Jump, on the road from Tavistock to Plymouth.

Sir Francis, according to tradition, was enabled to destroy the Spanish Armada by the aid of the devil. The old admiral went to Devil's Point, a well-known promontory jutting into Plymouth Sound. He there cut pieces of wood into the water, and by the power of magic and the assistance of his demon these became at once well armed gunboats.

The Queen, Elizabeth, gave Sir Francis Drake Buckland Abbey; and on every hand we hear of Drake and his familiars.

An extensive building attached to the Abbey – which was no doubt used as barns and stables after the place had been deprived of its religious character – was said to have been built by the devil in three nights. After the first night, the butler, astonished at the work done, resolved to watch and see how it was performed. Consequently, on the second night, he mounted into a large tree and hid himself behind the forks of its five branches. At midnight the devil came, driving several teams of oxen and, as some of them were lazy, he plucked this tree from the ground and used it as a goad. The poor butler lost his senses and never recovered them.

Drake constructed the channel, carrying the waters from Dartmoor to Plymouth. Tradition says he went with his demon to Dartmoor, walked into Plymouth, and the waters followed him. Even now – as old Betty Donnithorne, formerly the housekeeper at Buckland Abbey, told me – if the warrior hears the drum which hangs in the hall of the Abbey, and which accompanied him round the world, he rises and has a revel.

Some few years since, a small box was found in a closet which had long been closed, containing, it is supposed, family papers. This was sent to the residence of the inheritor of this property. The carriage was at the Abbey door, and a man easily lifted the box into it. The owner having taken his seat, the coachman attempted to start his horses, but in vain.

More horses were brought, and then the heavy farm-horses, and eventually all the oxen. They were powerless to start the carriage. At length a mysterious voice was heard, declaring that the box could never be moved from Buckland Abbey. It was taken from the carriage easily by one man, and a pair of horses galloped off with the carriage.

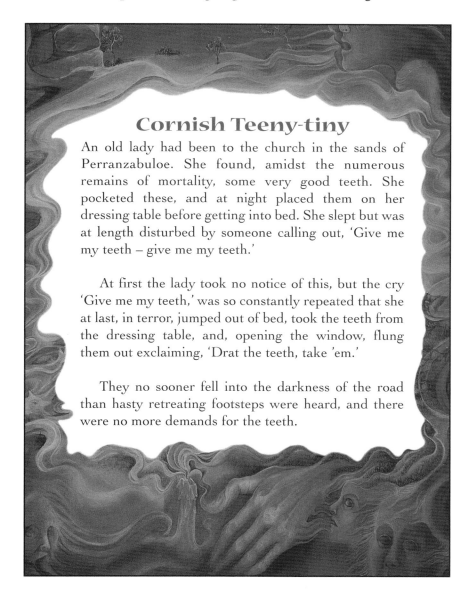

Cornish Teeny-tiny

An old lady had been to the church in the sands of Perranzabuloe. She found, amidst the numerous remains of mortality, some very good teeth. She pocketed these, and at night placed them on her dressing table before getting into bed. She slept but was at length disturbed by someone calling out, 'Give me my teeth – give me my teeth.'

At first the lady took no notice of this, but the cry 'Give me my teeth,' was so constantly repeated that she at last, in terror, jumped out of bed, took the teeth from the dressing table, and, opening the window, flung them out exclaiming, 'Drat the teeth, take 'em.'

They no sooner fell into the darkness of the road than hasty retreating footsteps were heard, and there were no more demands for the teeth.

The mermaid of Seaton

Near Looe – that is, between Down Derry and Looe – there is a little sand-beach called Seaton. Tradition tells us that here once stood a goodly commercial town bearing this name, and that when it was in its pride, Plymouth was but a small fishing-village.

The town of Seaton is said to have been overwhelmed with sand at an early period, the catastrophe having been brought about – as in the case of the filling up of Padstow harbour – by the curse of a mermaid, who had suffered some injury from the sailors who belonged to this port. Beyond this I have been unable to glean any story worth preserving.

The Hack and the Cast

In the parish of Goran is an intrenchment running from cliff to cliff, and cutting off about a hundred acres of coarse ground. This is about twenty feet broad, and twenty-four feet high in most places.

Marvellous as it may appear, tradition assures us that this was the work of a giant, and that he performed the task in a single night. This fortification has long been known a *Thica Vosa*, and the Hack and Cast. The giant, who lived on the promontory, was the terror of the neighbourhood, and great were the rejoicings in Goran when his death was accomplished through a stratagem by a neighbouring doctor.

The giant fell ill through eating some food – children or otherwise – to satisfy his voracity, which had disturbed his stomach. His roars and groans were heard for miles, and great was the terror throughout the neighbourhood. A messenger, however, soon arrived at the residence of the doctor of the parish, and he bravely resolved to obey the summons of the giant, and visit him. He found the giant rolling on the ground with pain, and he at once determined to rid the world, if possible, of the monster.

He told him that he must be bled. The giant submitted, and the doctor moreover said that, to insure relief, a large hole in the cliff must be filled with the blood. The giant lay on the ground, his arm extended over the hole, and the blood flowing a torrent into it. Relieved by the loss of blood, he permitted the stream to flow on, until he at last became so weak, that the doctor kicked him over the cliff, and killed him. The well-known promontory of The Dead Man, or Dodman, is so called from the dead giant. The spot on which he fell is the 'Giant's House', and the hole has ever since been most favourable to the growth of ivy.

The Spectral Coach

The old vicarage house at Talland, as seen from the Looe road, its low roof and grey walls peeping prettily from between the dense boughs of ash and elm that environed it, was as picturesque an object as you could desire to see. The seclusion of its situation was enhanced by the character of the house itself. It was an odd-looking, old-fashioned building, erected apparently in an age when ascetism and self-denial were more in vogue than at present, with a stern disregard of the comfort of the inhabitant, and in utter contempt of received principles of taste. As if not secure enough in its retirement, a high wall, enclosing a curtilage in front, effectually protected its inmates from the prying passenger, and only revealed the upper part of the house with its small Gothic windows, its slated roof, and heavy chimneys partly hidden by the evergreen shrubs which grew in the enclosure. Such was it until its removal a few years since; and such was it as it lay sweetly in the shadows of an autumnal evening one hundred and thirty years ago, when a stranger in the garb of a country labourer knocked hesitatingly at the wicket gate which conducted to the court. After a little delay a servant girl appeared, and finding that the countryman bore a message to the vicar, admitted him within the walls and conducted him along a paved passage to the little, low, damp parlour where sat the good man.

The Rev. Mr Dodge was in many respects a remarkable man. You would have judged as much of him as he sat before the fire in his high-back chair, in an attitude of thought, arranging, it may have been, the heads of his next Sabbath's discourse. His heavy eyebrows throwing into shade his spacious eyes, and indeed the whole contour of his face, marked him as a man of great firmness of character and of much moral and personal courage. His suit of sober black and full-bottomed periwig also added to his dignity, and gave him an appearance of greater age. He was then verging on sixty. The time and the place gave him abundant exercise for the qualities we have mentioned, for many of his parishioners obtained their livelihood by the contraband trade, and were mostly men of unscrupulous and daring character, little likely to bear with patience reflections on the dishonesty of their calling. Nevertheless the vicar was fearless in reprehending it, and his frank exhortations were, at least, listened to on account of the simple honesty of the man, and his well-known kindness of heart. The eccentricity of his life, too, had a wonderful effect in procuring him the respect, not to say the awe, of a people superstitious in a more than ordinary degree. Ghosts in those days had more freedom accorded them, or had more business with the visible world, than at present, and the parson was frequently required by his parishioners to draw from the uneasy spirit the dread secret which troubled it, or by the aid of the solemn prayers of the church to set it at rest for ever. Mr Dodge had a fame as an exorcist which was not confined to the bounds of his parish, nor limited to the age in which he lived.

'Well, my good man, what brings you hither?' said the clergyman to the messenger.

'A letter, may it please your reverence, from Mr Mills of Lanreath,' said the countryman, handing him a letter. Mr Dodge opened it and read as follows:

My dear brother Dodge,

I have ventured to trouble you at the earnest request of my parishioners, with a matter of which some particulars have doubtless reached you, and which has caused and is causing much terror in my neighbourhood. For its fuller explication, I will be so tedious as to recount to you the whole of this strange story as it has reached my ears, for as yet I have not satisfied my eyes with its truth. It has been told to me by men of honest and good report (witnesses of a portion of what they relate), with such strong assurances that it behoves us to look more closely into the matter. There is in the neighbourhood of this village a barren bit of moor which had no owner, or rather more than one, for the lords of the adjoining manors debated its ownership between themselves, and both determined to take it from the poor, who have for many years regarded it as a common. And truly, it is little to the credit of these gentlemen that they should strive for a thing so worthless as scarce to bear the cost of law, and yet of no mean value to poor labouring people. The two litigants, however, contested it with as much violence as if it had been a field of great price, and especially one, an old man (whose thoughts should have been less set on earthly possessions, which he was soon to leave), had so set his heart of the success of his suit, that the loss of it, a few years back, is said to have much hastened his death. Nor, indeed, after death, if current reports are worthy of credit, does he quit his claim to it; for at night-time his apparition is seen on the moor, to the great terror of the neighbouring villagers. A public path leads by at no great distance from the spot, and on divers [several] occasions has the labourer, returning from his work, been frightened nigh unto lunacy by sight and sounds of a very dreadful character. The appearance is said to be that of a man habited in black, driving a carriage drawn by headless horses. This is, I avow, very marvellous to believe, but it has had so much credible testimony, and has gained so many believers in my parish, that some steps may seem necessary to allay the excitement it causes. I have been applied to for this purpose, and my present business is to ask your assistance in this matter, either to reassure the minds of the country people, if it be only a simple terror; or, if there be truth in it, to set the troubled spirit of the man at rest. My messenger, who is an industrious, trusty man, will give you more information if it be needed, for, from report, he is acquainted with most of the circumstances, and will bring back your advice and promise of assistance.

Not doubting of your help herein, I do, with my very hearty commendation, commit you to God's protection and blessing, and am,

Your very loving brother

Abraham Mills

This remarkable note was read and re-read, while the countryman sat watching its effects on the parson's countenance and surprised that it changed not from its usual sedate and settled character.

Turning at length to the man, Mr Dodge inquired, 'Are you, then, acquainted with my good friend Mills?'

'I should know him, sir,' replied the messenger, 'having been sexton to the parish for fourteen years, and being, with my family, much beholden to the kindness of the rector.'

'You are also not without some knowledge of the circumstances related in this letter. Have you been an eyewitness to any of those strange sights?'

'For myself, sir, I have been on the road at all hours of the night and day, and never did I see anything which I would call worse than myself. One night my wife and I were awoke by the rattle of wheels, which was also heard by some of our neighbours, and we were all assured that it could have been no other than the black coach. We have every day such stories told in the villages by so many creditable persons, that it would not be proper in a plain, ignorant man like me to doubt it.'

'And how far,' asked the clergyman, 'is the moor from Lanreath?'

'About two miles, and please your reverence. The whole parish is so frightened that few will venture far after nightfall, for it has of late come much nearer the village. A man who is esteemed a sensible and pious man by many, though an Anabaptist in principle, went a few weeks back to the moor ('tis called Blackadon) at midnight, in order to lay the spirit, being requested thereto by his neighbours, and he was so alarmed by what he saw that he hath been somewhat mazed ever since.'

'A fitting punishment for his presumption, if it hath not quite demented him,' said the parson. 'These persons are like those addressed by St Chrysostom, fitly called the golden-mouthed, who said, "Miserable wretches that ye be! ye cannot expel a flea, much less a devil!" It will be well if it serves no other purpose but to bring back these stray sheep to

the fold of the Church. So this story has gained much belief in the parish?'
'

Most believe it, sir, as rightly they should, what hath so many witnesses,' said the sexton, 'though there be some, chiefly young men, who set up for being wiser than their fathers and refuse to credit it, though it be sworn on the book.'

'If those things are disbelieved, friend,' said the parson, 'and without inquiry, which your disbeliever is ever the first to shrink from, of what worth is human testimony? That ghosts have returned to the earth, either for the discovery of murder, or to make restitution for other injustice committed in the flesh, or compelled thereto by the incantations of sorcery, or to communicate tidings from another world, has been testified to in all ages, and many are the accounts which have been left us both in sacred and profane authors. Did not Brutus, when in Asia, as is related by Plutarch, see...'

Just at this moment the parson's handmaid announced that a person waited on him in the kitchen, or the good clergyman would probably have detailed all those cases in history, general and biblical, with which his reading had acquainted him, not much, we fear, to the edification or comfort of the sexton, who had to return to Lanreath, a long and dreary road after nightfall. So, instead, he directed the girl to take him with her, and give him such refreshment as he needed, and in the meanwhile he prepared a note in answer to Mr Mills, informing him that on the morrow he was to visit some sick persons in his parish, but that on the following evening he should be ready to proceed with him to the moor.

On the night appointed the two clergymen left the Lanreath rectory on horseback, and reached the moor at eleven o'clock. Bleak and dismal did it look by day, but then there was the distant landscape dotted over with pretty homesteads to relieve its desolation. Now, nothing was seen but the black patch of sterile moor, on which they stood, nothing heard but the wind as it swept in gusts across the bare hill, and howled dismally through a stunted grove of trees that grew in the glen below them, except the occasional baying of dogs from the farmhouses in the distance.

That they felt at ease is more than could be expected of them; but as it would have shown a lack of faith in the protection of heaven, which it would have been unseemly in men of the holy calling to exhibit, they managed to conceal from each other their uneasiness. Leading their horses, they trod to and fro through the damp fern and heath with firmness in their steps, and upheld each other by remarks on the power of that Great Being whose ministers they were, and the might of whose name they were there to make manifest. Still slowly and dismally passed the time as they conversed, and anon stopped to look through the darkness for the approach of their ghostly visitor. In vain. Though the night was as dark and murky as ghost could wish, the coach and its driver came not.

After a considerable stay, the two clergymen consulted together and determined that it was useless to watch any longer for that night, but they would meet on some other, when perhaps it might please his ghostship to appear. Accordingly, with a few words of leave-taking, they separated, Mr Mills for the rectory, and Mr Doble, by a short ride across the moor, which shortened his journey by half a mile, for the vicarage at Talland.

The vicar rode on at an ambling pace, which his good mare sustained up hill and down dale without urging. At the bottom of a deep valley, however, about a mile from Blackadon, the animal became very uneasy, pricked up her ears, snorted, and moved from side to side of the road, as if something stood in the path before her. The parson tightened the reins, and applied whip and spur to her sides, but the animal, usually docile, became very unruly, made several attempts to turn, and, when prevented, threw herself upon her haunches. Whip and spur were applied again and again, to no other purpose than to add to the horse's terror.

To the rider nothing was apparent which could account for the sudden restiveness of his beast. He dismounted and attempted in turns to lead or drag her, but both were impracticable, and attended with no small risk of snapping the reins. She was remounted with great difficulty, and another attempt was made to urge her forward, with the like want of success. At length the eccentric clergyman, judging it to be some special signal from heaven, which it would be dangerous to neglect, threw the reins on the neck of his steed, which, wheeling suddenly round, started backward in a direction towards the moor, at a pace which rendered the parson's seat neither a pleasant nor a safe one. In an astonishingly short space of time they were once more at Blackadon.

By this time the bare outline of the moor was broken by a large black group of objects, which the darkness of the night prevented the parson from defining. On approaching this unaccountable appearance, the mare was seized with fresh fury, and it was with considerable difficulty that she could be brought to face this new cause of fright. In the pauses of the horse's prancing, the vicar discovered to his horror the much-dreaded spectacle of the black coach and the headless steeds, and, terrible to relate, his friend Mr Mills lying prostrate upon the ground before the sable driver. Little time was left him to call up his courage for this fearful emergency; for just as the vicar began to give utterance to the earnest prayers which struggled to his lips, the spectre shouted, 'Dodge is come! I must be gone!' and forthwith leapt into his chariot and disappeared across the moor.

The fury of the mare now subsided, and Mr Dodge was enabled to approach his friend who was lying motionless and speechless, with his face buried in the heather.

Meanwhile the rector's horse, which had taken fright at the apparition, and had thrown his rider to the ground on or near the spot where we have left him lying, made homeward at a furious speed and stopped not until he had reached his stable door. The sound of his hoofs as he galloped madly through the village awoke the cottagers, many of whom had been some hours in their beds. Many eager faces, staring with affright, gathered round the rectory and added, by their various conjectures, to the terror and apprehension of the family.

The villagers, gathering courage as their numbers increased, agreed to go in search of the missing clergyman, and started off in a compact body, a few on horseback but the greater number on foot, in the direction of Blackadon.

There they discovered their rector, supported in the arms of Parson Dodge and recovered so far as to be able to speak. Still there was a wildness in his eye and an incoherency in his speech that showed that his reason was, at least temporarily, unsettled by the fright. In this condition he was taken to his home, followed by his reverend companion.

Here ended this strange adventure; for Mr Mills soon completely regained his reason, Parson Dodge got safely back to Talland, and from that time to this nothing has been heard or seen of the black ghost or his chariot.

The Haunted Widower

A labouring man, very shortly after his wife's death, sent to a servant girl living at the time in a small shipping port, requesting her to come to the inn to him. The girl went, and over a 'ha' pint' she agreed to accept him as her husband.

All went on pleasantly enough for a time. One evening the man met the girl. He was silent for some time and sorrowful, but at length he told her his wife had come back.

'What do'st mean?' asked the girl. 'Have 'e seen hur?'
'Naw, I han't seed her.'
'Why, how do'st knaw it is her then?'

The poor man explained to her that at night, when in bed, she would come to the side of it and 'flop' his face; and there was no mistaking her 'flop'.

'So you knawed her flop, did 'e?' asked the girl.
'Ay, it couldn't be mistook.'

'If she do hunt thee,' said the girl, 'she'll hunt me; and if she do flop 'e, she'll flop me – so it must be off atween us.'

The unfortunate flop of the dead wife prevented the man from securing a living one.

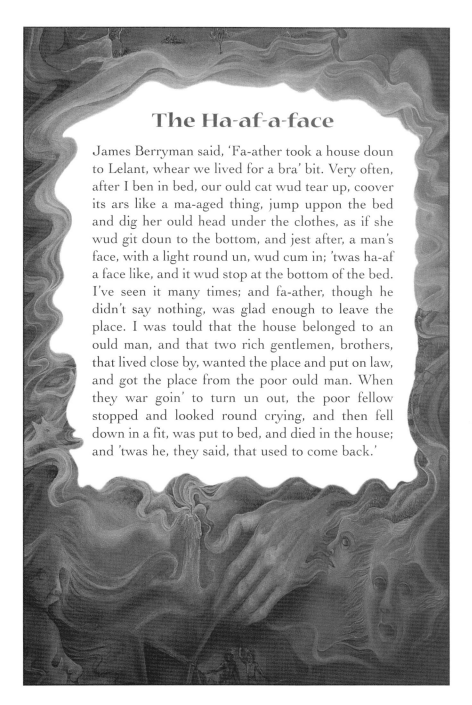

The Ha-af-a-face

James Berryman said, 'Fa-ather took a house doun to Lelant, whear we lived for a bra' bit. Very often, after I ben in bed, our ould cat wud tear up, coover its ars like a ma-aged thing, jump uppon the bed and dig her ould head under the clothes, as if she wud git doun to the bottom, and jest after, a man's face, with a light round un, wud cum in; 'twas ha-af a face like, and it wud stop at the bottom of the bed. I've seen it many times; and fa-ather, though he didn't say nothing, was glad enough to leave the place. I was tould that the house belonged to an ould man, and that two rich gentlemen, brothers, that lived close by, wanted the place and put on law, and got the place from the poor ould man. When they war goin' to turn un out, the poor fellow stopped and looked round crying, and then fell down in a fit, was put to bed, and died in the house; and 'twas he, they said, that used to come back.'

Who are the Knockers?

Many a time have I been seriously informed by the miners themselves that these sprites have been heard working away in the remote parts of a lode, repeating the blows of the miner's pick or sledge with great precision. Generally speaking, the knockers work on productive lodes only, and they have often kindly indicated to the trusting miners where they might take good tribute pitches.

One Saturday night I had retired to rest, having first seen that all the members of the household had gone to their bedrooms. These were my daughters, two female servants and an old woman named Mary, who was left by the proprietor in charge of the house which I occupied.

I had been some time in bed when I distinctly heard a bedroom door open and footsteps which, after moving about for some time in the passage or landing, from which the bedrooms opened, slowly and carefully descended the stairs. I heard a movement in the kitchen below, and the footsteps again ascended the stairs and went into one of the bedrooms. This noise continued so long, and was so regularly repeated, that I began to fear lest one of the children were taken suddenly ill. Yet I felt assured, if it was so, one of the servants would call me. Therefore I lay still and listened until I fell asleep.

On the Sunday morning, when I descended to the breakfast-room, I asked the eldest of the two servants what had occasioned so much going up and down stairs in the night. She declared that no one had left their bedrooms after they had retired to them. I then inquired of the younger girl, and of each of my daughters as they made their appearance. No one had left their rooms – they had not heard any noises.

My youngest daughter, who had been after this inquiry of mine for some minutes alone with the youngest servant, came laughing to me.

'Papa, Nancy says the house is haunted and that they have often heard strange noises in it.'

So I called Nancy; but all I could learn from her was that noises, like men going up and down stairs, of threshing corn and 'beating the borer' (a mining operation) were not uncommon.

We all laughed over papa's ghost during the breakfast, and by and by old Mary made her appearance.

'Yes,' she said, 'it is quite true, as Nancy 'as a-told you. I have often heard all sorts of strange noises; but I b'lieve they all come from the lode of tin which runs under the house. Wherever there is a lode of tin, you are sure to hear strange noises.'

'What, Mary! was it the knockers I heard last night?'

'Yes, 'twas the knackers, down working upon the tin – no doubt of it.'

This was followed by a long explanation, and numerous stories of mines in the Lelant and St Ives district, in which the knockers had often been heard.

After a little time, Mary, imagining I suppose that the young ladies might not like to sleep in a house beneath which the knockers were at work, again came with her usual low courtsey into the parlour.

'Beg pardon, sir,' says she, 'but none of the young ladies need be afraid. There are no spirits in the house; it is very nearly a new one, and no one has ever died in the house.'

This makes a distinct difference between the ghost of the departed and those gnomes who are doomed to toil in the earth's dark recesses.

The Spectre Bridegroom

Long long ago a farmer named Lenine lived in Boscean. He had but one son, Frank Lenine, who was indulged into waywardness by both his parents. In addition to the farm servants, there was one, a young girl, Nancy Trenoweth, who especially assisted Mrs Lenine in all the various duties of a small farmhouse.

Nancy Trenoweth was very pretty, and although perfectly uneducated in the sense in which we now employ the term education, she possessed many native graces and she had acquired much knowledge really useful to one whose aspirations would probably never rise higher than to be mistress of a farm of a few acres. Educated by parents who had certainly never seen the world beyond Penzance, her ideas of the world were limited to a few miles around the Land's End. But although her book of nature was a small one, it had deeply impressed her mind with its influences. The wild waste, the small but fertile valley, the rugged hills with their crowns of cairns, the moors rich in the golden furze and the purple heath, the sea-beaten cliffs, and the silver sands, were the pages she had studied, under the guidance of a mother who conceived, in the sublimity of her ignorance, that everything in nature was the home of some spirit form. The soul of the girl was imbued with the deeply religious dye of her mother's mind, whose religion was only a sense of an unknown world immediately beyond our own. The elder Nancy Trenoweth exerted over the villagers around her considerable power. They did not exactly fear her. She was too free from evil for that. But they were conscious of a mental superiority and yielded without complaining to her sway.

The result of this was that the younger Nancy, although compelled to service, always exhibited some pride, from a feeling that her mother was a superior woman to any around her.

She never felt herself inferior to her master and mistress, yet she complained not of being in subjection to them. There were so many interesting features in the character of this young servant girl that she became in many respects like a daughter to her mistress. There was no broad line of division in those days, in even the manorial hall, between the lord and his domestics, and still less defined was the position of the employed and the employer in a small farmhouse. Consequent upon this condition of things, Frank Lenine and Nancy were thrown as much together as if they had been brother and sister. Frank was rarely checked in anything by his over-fond parents, who were especially proud of their son since he was regarded as the handsomest young man in the parish. Frank conceived a very warm attachment to Nancy, and she was not a little proud of her lover. Although it was evident to all the parish that Frank and Nancy were seriously devoted to each other, the young man's parents were blind to it and were taken by surprise when one day Frank asked his father and mother to consent to his marrying Nancy.

The Lenines had allowed their son to have his own way from his youth up; and now, in a matter which brought into play the strongest of human feelings, they were angry because he refused to bend to their wills.

The old man felt it would be a degradation for a Lenine to marry a Trenoweth and, in a most unreasoning manner, he resolved it should never be.

The first act was to send Nancy home to Alsia Mill where her parents resided; the next was an imperious command to his son never again to see the girl.

The commands of the old are generally powerless upon the young where the affairs of the heart are concerned. So were they upon Frank. He, who was rarely seen of an evening beyond the garden of his father's cottage, was now as constantly absent from his home. The house, which was wont to be a pleasant one, was strangely altered. A gloom had fallen over all things; the father and the son rarely met as friends, the mother and her boy had now a feeling of reserve. Often there were angry altercations between the father and son, and the mother felt she could not become the defender of her boy in his open acts of disobedience, his bold defiance of his parents' commands.

Rarely an evening passed that did not find Nancy and Frank together in some retired nook. The Holy Well was a favourite meeting place, and here the most solemn vows were made. Locks of hair were exchanged; a wedding-ring, taken from the finger of a corpse, was broken when they vowed that they would be united either dead or alive; and they even climbed at night the granite pile at Treryn, and swore by the Logan Rock the same strong vow.

Time passed onward thus unhappily and, as a result of the endeavours to quench out the passion by force, it grew stronger under the repressing power, and like imprisoned steam eventually burst through all restraint.

Nancy's parents discovered at length that moonlight meetings between two untrained, impulsive youths had a natural result and they were now doubly earnest to compel Frank to marry their daughter.

The elder Lenine could not be brought to consent to this, and he firmly resolved to remove his son entirely from what he considered the hateful influences of the Trenoweths. He resolved to go to Plymouth, to take his son with him, and if possible to send him away to sea, hoping thus to wean him from his folly, as he considered this love madness. Frank, poor fellow, with the best intentions was not capable of any sustained effort, and consequently he at length succumbed to his father; and to escape his persecution he entered a ship bound for India, and bade adieu to his native land.

Frank could not write, and this happened in days when letters could be forwarded only with extreme difficulty; consequently Nancy never heard from her lover.

A baby had been born into this troublesome world, and the infant became a real solace to the young mother. As the child grew, it became an especial favourite with its grandmother; the elder Nancy rejoiced over the little prattler and forgot her cause of sorrow. Young Nancy lived for her child, and on the memory of its father. Subdued in spirit she was, but her affliction had given force to her character, and she had been heard to declare that wherever Frank was she was ever present with him; whatever might be the temptations of the hour, that her influence was all-powerful over him for good. She felt that no distance could separate their souls, that no time could be long enough to destroy the bond between them.

A period of distress fell upon the Trenoweths, and it was necessary that Nancy should leave her home once more and go again into service. Her mother took charge of the babe, and she found a situation in Kemyel, in the parish of Paul. Nancy, like her mother, contrived to maintain an ascendancy amongst her companions. She had formed an acquaintance, which certainly never grew into friendship, with some of the daughters of the small farmers around. These girls were all full of the superstitions of the time and place.

The winter was coming on and nearly three years had passed away since Frank Lenine had left his country. As yet there was no sign. Nor father nor mother nor maiden had heard of him, and they all sorrowed over his absence. The Lenines desired to have Nancy's child, but the Trenoweths would not part with it. They went so far even as to endeavour to persuade Nancy to live again with them, but Nancy was not at all disposed to submit to their wishes.

It was All-hallows Eve, and two of Nancy's companions persuaded her – no very difficult task – to go with them and sow hemp-seed.

At midnight the three maidens stole out unperceived into Kemyel town-place to perform their incantation. Nancy was the first to sow, the others being less bold than she. Boldly she advanced, saying as she scattered the seed,

'Hemp-seed I sow thee,
Hemp-seed grow thee;
And he who will my true love be,
Come after me,
And shaw thee.'

This was repeated three times, when, looking back over her left shoulder, she saw Lenine; but he looked so angry that she shrieked with fear and broke the spell. One of the other girls, however, resolved now to make trial of the spell, and the result of her labours was the vision of a white coffin. Fear now fell on all, and they went home sorrowful, to spend each one a sleepless night.

November came with its storms, and during one terrific night a large vessel was thrown upon the rocks in Burnewhall Cliff and, beaten by impetuous waves, she was soon in pieces. Amongst the bodies of the crew washed ashore, nearly all of whom had perished, was Frank Lenine. He was not dead when found, but the only words he lived to speak were begging the people to send for Nancy Trenoweth, that he might make her his wife before he died.

Rapidly sinking, Frank was borne by his friends on a litter to Boscean, but he died as he reached the town-place.

His parents, overwhelmed in their own sorrows, thought nothing of Nancy and, without her knowing that Lenine had returned, the poor fellow was laid to his last bed in Buryan churchyard.

On the night of the funeral, Nancy went as was her custom to lock the door of the house, and, as was her custom too, she looked out into the night. At this instant a horseman rode up in haste, called her by name, and hailed her in a voice that made her blood boil.

The voice was the voice of Lenine. She could never forget that; and the horse she now saw was her sweetheart's favourite colt, on which he had often ridden at night to Alsia.

The rider was imperfectly seen, but he looked very sorrowful, and deadly pale; still, Nancy knew him to be Frank Lenine.

He told her that he had just arrived home, and that the first moment he was at liberty he had taken horse to fetch his beloved one and to make her his bride.

Nancy's excitement was so great that she was easily persuaded to spring on the horse behind him, that they might reach his home before the morning.

When she took Lenine's hand a cold shiver passed through her, and as she grasped his waist to secure herself in her seat, her arm became as stiff as ice. She lost all power of speech and suffered deep fear, yet she knew not why. The moon had arisen, and now burst out in a full flood of light through the heavy clouds which had obscured it. The horse pursued its journey with great rapidity, and whenever in weariness it slackened its speed, the peculiar voice of the rider aroused its drooping energies. Beyond this no word was spoken since Nancy had mounted behind her lover. They now came to Trove Bottom, where there was no bridge at that time; they dashed into the river. The moon shone full in their faces. Nancy looked into the stream and saw that the rider was in a shroud and other grave-clothes. She now knew that she was being carried away by a spirit, yet she had no power to save herself; indeed, the inclination to do so did not exist.

On went the horse at a furious pace, until they came to the blacksmith's shop near Buryan Church-town, when she knew by the light of the forge-fire thrown across the road that the smith was still at his labours. She now recovered speech. 'Save me! save me! save me!' she cried with all her might. The smith sprang from the door of the smithy, with a red-hot iron in his hand, and as the horse rushed by caught the woman's dress and pulled her to the ground. The spirit, however, also seized Nancy's dress in one hand and his grasp was like that of a vice. The horse passed like the wind, and Nancy and the smith were pulled down as far as the old almshouses, near the church-yard. Here the horse for a moment stopped. The smith seized that moment, and with his hot iron burned off the dress from the rider's hand, thus saving Nancy, more dead than alive; while the rider passed over the wall of the churchyard and vanished on the grave in which Lenine had been laid but hours before.

The smith took Nancy into his shop, and he soon aroused some of his neighbours, who took the poor girl back to Alsia. Her parents laid her on her bed. She spoke no word, but to ask for her child, to request her mother to give up her child to Lenine's parents, and her desire to be buried in his grave. Before the morning light fell on the world, Nancy had breathed her last breath.

A horse was seen that night to pass through the Church-town like a ball from a musket, and in the morning Lenine's colt was found dead in Burnewhall Cliff, covered with foam, its eyes forced from its head and its swollen tongue hanging out of its mouth. On Lenine's grave was found the piece of Nancy's dress which was left in the spirit's hand when the smith burnt her from his grasp.

It is said that one or two of the sailors who survived the wreck related after the funeral how, on 30 October at night, Lenine was like one mad; they could scarcely keep him in the ship. He seemed more asleep than awake and, after great excitement, he fell as if dead upon the deck and lay so for hours. When he came to himself, he told them he had been taken to the village of Kemyel, and that if he ever married the woman who had cast the spell, he would make her suffer the longest day she had to live for drawing his soul out of his body.

Poor Nancy was buried in Lenine's grave, and her companion in sowing hemp-seed, who saw the white coffin, slept beside her within the year.

Pengerswick Castle

This castellated building – for it does not now admit of being called a castle, notwithstanding its embattled turrets and its machicolated gate – is situated in a hollow running down to Pengerswick Cove, in the Mount's Bay, where there never could have been anything to defend; and certainly there is nothing to induce any one to incur the cost of such a building.

Mr Milliton, in the reign of Henry VIII, slew in the streets of London a man in a drunken brawl. He fled, and went to sea. It is not known to what part of the world he went, but we are told that he became excessively rich; so rich, indeed, that 'when he loaded his ass with his gold, the weight was so great as to break the poor animal's back.' Returning to his country, and not daring to appear in any of the large towns, he bought the manor of Pengerswick, and built this castle, to defend himself, in the event of his being approached by any of the officers of the law.

A miserable man, Milliton is said to have lived in a secret chamber in this tower, and to have been visited only by his most trusted friends. Deeply deploring the crime that had condemned him to seclusion from the world, he spent his dreary hours in ornamenting his dwelling. His own story is supposed to be told in the painting of an overladen ass in one room, with a black-letter legend, importing that a miser is like an ass loaded with riches, who, without attending to his golden burden, feeds on thistles.

There is also a carving of water wearing a hollow in a stone, and under it the word 'Perseverance'. Of the death of Milliton we have no account.

There is very little doubt but that Pengerswick Castle is very much older than the time of Milliton; indeed tradition informs us that he purchased the place. The legends previously given, and others in my possession, refer to a much earlier period. The castle was, it is said, surrounded by trees; but John Hals, who inherited the property, had all the timber cut down and sold.

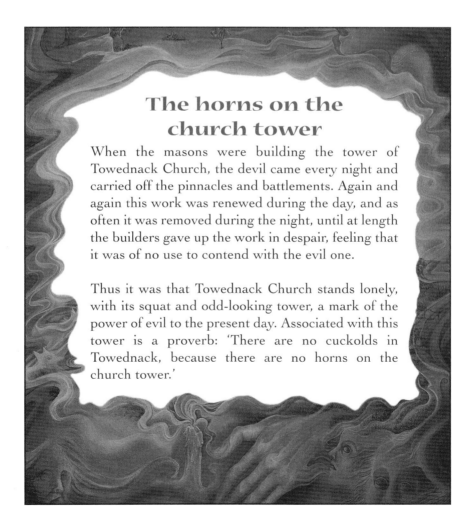

The horns on the church tower

When the masons were building the tower of Towednack Church, the devil came every night and carried off the pinnacles and battlements. Again and again this work was renewed during the day, and as often it was removed during the night, until at length the builders gave up the work in despair, feeling that it was of no use to contend with the evil one.

Thus it was that Towednack Church stands lonely, with its squat and odd-looking tower, a mark of the power of evil to the present day. Associated with this tower is a proverb: 'There are no cuckolds in Towednack, because there are no horns on the church tower.'

The old custom of....
Crying the Neck

Owing to the uncertain character of the climate of Cornwall, the farmers have adopted the plan of gathering the sheaves of wheat, as speedily as possible, into 'arishmows'. These are solid cones from ten to twelve feet high, the heads of the stalks turned inwards, and the whole capped with a sheaf of corn inverted. Whence the term, I know not; but 'arish' is commonly applied to a field of corn recently cut, as, 'Turn the geese in upon the arish' - that is, the short stubble left in the ground.

After the wheat is all cut on most farms in Cornwall and Devon, the harvest people have a custom of 'crying the neck'. I believe that this practice is seldom omitted on any large farm in these counties. It is done in this way. An old man, or some one else well acquainted with the ceremonies used on the occasion (when the labourers are reaping the last field of wheat), goes round to the shocks and sheaves, and picks out a little bundle of all the best ears he can find; this bundle he ties up very neat and trim, and plaits and arranges the straws very tastefully. This is called 'the neck' of wheat, or wheaten-ears.

After the field is cut out, and the pitcher once more circulated, the reapers, binders, and the women stand round in a circle. The person with 'the neck' stands in the centre, grasping it with both his hands. He first stoops and holds it near the ground, and all the men forming the ring take off their hats, stooping and holding them with both hands towards the ground. They then all begin at once, in a very prolonged and harmonious tone, to cry, 'The neck!' at the same time slowly raising themselves upright, and elevating their arms and hats above their heads; the person with the neck also raising it on high. This is done three times. They then change their cry to 'We yen! we yen!' which they sound in the same prolonged and slow manner as before, with singular harmony and effect, three times. This last cry is accompanied by the same movements of the body and arms as in crying 'the neck'.

Well, after this they all burst out into a kind of loud, joyous laugh, flinging up their hats and caps into the air, capering about, and perhaps kissing the girls. One of them then gets 'the neck', and runs as hard as he can down to the farmhouse, where the dairy-maid, or one of the young female domestics, stands at the door prepared with a pail of water. If he who holds 'the neck' can manage to get into the house in any way unseen, or openly by any other way than the door at which the girl stands with the pail of water, then he may lawfully kiss her; but if otherwise, he is regularly soused with the contents of the bucket. I think this practice is beginning to decline of late, and many farmers and their men do not care about keeping up this old custom. The object of crying 'the neck' is to give notice to the surrounding country of the end of the harvest, and the meaning of 'we yen' is 'we have ended'. It may probably mean 'we end', which the uncouth and provincial pronunciation has corrupted into 'we yen'. The 'neck' is generally hung up in the farmhouse, where it often remains for three or four years.

....Sham Mayor

There was a curious custom in the town of Penryn in Cornwall, which long outlived all modern innovations. On some particular day in September or October, about when the hazel-nuts are ripe, the festival of nutting-day is kept. The rabble of the town go into the country to gather nuts, returning in the evening with boughs of hazel in their hands, shouting and making a great noise. In the meantime the journeymen tailors of the town have proceeded to the adjoining village of Mylor, and elected one of their number 'Mayor of Mylor', taking care the selection falls on the wittiest.

Seated in a chair shaded with green boughs, and borne on the shoulders of four stalwart men, the worthy mayor proceeds from his 'good town of Mylor' to his 'ancient borough of Penryn', the van being led by the 'bodyguard' of stout fellows well armed with cudgels (which they do not fail to use should their path be obstructed), torch-bearers, and two 'town serjeants', clad in official gowns and cocked hats, and carrying each a monstrous cabbage on his shoulder in lieu of a mace. The rear is brought up by the rabble of the 'nutters'.

About mid-day a band of music meets them, and plays them to Penryn, where they are received by the entire population. The procession proceeds to the town-hall, in front of which the mayor delivers a speech, declaratory of his intended improvements for the coming year, being generally an excellent sarcastic burlesque on the speeches of parliamentary candidates. The procession then moves on to each public-house door, where the mayor, his council, and officers, are liberally supplied with liquor, and the speech is repeated with variations. They then adjourn to the 'council-chamber', in some public-house, and devote the night to drinking.

At night the streets are filled with people bearing torches, throwing fireballs, and discharging rockets; and huge bonfires are kindled on the Green, and Old Wall. The legal mayor once made an effort to put a stop to this saturnalia, but his new-made brother issued prompt orders to his bodyguards, and the *posse comitatus* (force of the country) had to fly. The popular opinion is that there is a clause in the borough charter compelling the legitimate mayor to surrender his power to the 'Mayor of Mylor' on the night in question, and to lend the town sergeants' paraphernalia to the gentlemen of the shears.

....Geese-dancing

The first Monday after Twelfth-day is Plough Monday, and it is the ploughman's holiday.

At this season, in the Islands of Scilly, at St Ives, Penzance, and other places, the young people exercise a sort of gallantry called 'geese-dancing'. The maidens are dressed up for young men, and the young men for maidens; and, thus disguised, they visit their neighbours in companies, where they dance, and make jokes upon what has happened during the year, and every one is humorously 'told their own', without offence being taken. By this sort of sport, according to yearly custom and toleration, there is a spirit of wit and drollery kept up among the people. The music and dancing done, they are treated with liquor, and then they go to the next house, and carry on the same sport. A correspondent, writing to the *Table-Book* insists on calling these revels 'goose-dancing'. The true Cornishman never uses the term, which is, as I have elsewhere shown, derived from *dance deguiser*, hence guise-dancing, or geese-dancing, by corruption.